BEAT THIS!
Cookbook

BEAT THIS!
Cookbook

By Ann Hodgman

Illustrations by Robin Zingone

CHAPTERS PUBLISHING, LTD., SHELBURNE, VERMONT 05482

Published by
Chapters Publishing Ltd.
2031 Shelburne Road
Shelburne, Vermont 05482

Library of Congress Cataloguing-in-Publication Data

Hodgman, Ann.
    Beat this! cookbook : the very best recipe for apple pie, brownies, crab cakes, deviled
eggs, french toast, guacamole, onion rings, potato salad, roast turkey, spaghetti sauce, stuffing,
strawberry shortcake, white chocolate raspberry pie, and more than 100 other "make-them-
stagger-with-joy" recipes / by Ann Hodgman ; illustrations by Robin Zingone
      p.   cm.
  Includes index.
  ISBN 1-881527-21-2 (pbk.) : $12.95.
  1. Cookery, American. I. Title.
TX715.H7233 1993
641.5973—dc20   93-25422
                                                      CIP

Trade distribution by
Firefly Books Ltd.
250 Sparks Avenue
Willowdale, Ontario
Canada M2H 2S4

Printed and bound in Canada by
Best Gagné Book Manufacturers, Inc.
Louiseville, Quebec

Designed by Impress, Inc., Northampton, Massachusetts

At last, one I can dedicate to David

Acknowledgments

Growing Up

My mother not only taught me a great deal about cooking, including how to make the perfect omelette, but cheerfully and repeatedly turned the kitchen over to me even though she knew I would not return it in good condition.

My father didn't throw up the time he came in from jogging on a roasting-hot summer evening and I, having just read a luscious description of hot chocolate in **My Friend Flicka**, presented him with a steaming mugful of it. He also never complained when I experimented with his bag lunches.

My sisters endured my merciless bossing whenever they stepped into the kitchen. My brother and his wife didn't kill me when I volunteered to make their wedding cake and it collapsed three hours before the wedding.

My godmother, Ruth Atwater; Charles and Hannah Solkey; Cornelia Hopfield; and Porter Perham were all inspirational cooks.

Saucy, The Queen of Dogs, cleaned up the floor when I spilled things.

New York

Rebecca Atwater was the best fellow foodie a person could have. Whenever I eat a bagel, I remember her pointing out that every bagel has a tiny bit of onion *somewhere*.

Irene Sax was (and is) a second mother to me in both emotional and culinary matters.

Ann Whitman introduced me to Cape Cod potato chips.

Shortie, The Next Queen of Dogs, cleaned up the floor when I spilled things and taught me that even a dachshund can reach food on the kitchen counter if she really wants to.

Washington, Connecticut

Kurt Andersen and Graydon Carter started this whole thing when they let me write about food for **Spy**.

Rux Martin and Barry Estabrook, my editors for this book, were endlessly patient, supportive and funny. Also, Rux's mother once had a pet woodchuck.

Michael Ackerman let me make chocolates for The Pantry, helped me find exotic ingredients when I needed them and gave excellent advice about suppliers.

Phil Gargan and Mike Condon taught me a lot about butchering. They also didn't flinch when I looked at the Big Boy saw in their butcher shop and commented, "Gee, that could cut your hand off in about two seconds."

The parishioners of St. John's Church were the cheerful guinea pigs for many of my cooking experiments.

Japan, my cockatiel, perched on my shoulder and dropped feathers into the mixing bowl during many late-night recipe-testing sessions.

As of this writing, Moxie, The Future Queen of Dogs, won't be born for another two weeks. But I'm sure she'll be just as good at cleaning up spilled food as her predecessors were.

Introduction

WHY ARE PEOPLE always so proud of their brownie recipes? Katharine Hepburn, for example. If there's anything I'm sick of—besides the way she always says she's a regular person and not an actress—it's reading about how sinful her brownies are. Actually, Hepburn's is the dullest brownie formula there is, and one of the most common. There's a copy of it in my daughter's nursery-school cookbook (prefaced by the remark, "These are sinful"); there's a copy of it in two different Junior League cookbooks I own; there's a copy of it in **Fannie Farmer**. All these recipes for an utterly undistinguished product! I guess sin is duller than I thought.

Brownies aren't the only food for which people always think their recipe is the best. Another one is meat loaf. Ann Landers gets hundreds of requests for her meat loaf recipe, which is strange considering that it, too, is ordinary in the extreme. (Ground meat, ketchup, onion soup mix—you get the picture.) There's a whole feedlot of recipes out there with self-awarded blue ribbons. But it's rare to find a "best" recipe that's even worth reading—much less eating.

Except for the ones in this book. These really *are* the best. There's just no point in trying any other recipes but these. I mean, there's just no point in trying any other recipes *for these foods* but these. What I mean is, these are the best recipes *of their type*. Well, you know what I mean. I guess I mean, if you're looking for a blini recipe, my chili recipe won't do you much good. But if you're looking for a chili recipe, it will. Know what I mean?

I'm not very good at coming up with original recipes, although my daughter Laura is. One of my favorites is one she composed when she was five:

Plain Dough
Sugar
Raisins
Any fruit
Cookit

Unlike Laura, I can't just walk into the kitchen and improvise a brilliant new dish. But I *can* figure out how to improve a recipe. I just double the chocolate and add some bacon.

Of course it's a little more complicated than that. Still, some of the recipes in this book wouldn't necessarily be considered healthy. Lots of them, I guess. But the best recipes are rarely the healthiest. When you're looking for the best potato salad to take to a potluck, or the best blueberry pie to bring to a bake sale, or—uh—the best French toast to serve to your boss at that breakfast meeting, you're not usually concerned with the dish's fat content. You just want people to take a bite, stagger with joy and beg you for the recipe.

With these recipes, they will. I know, because it always happens to me.

A word about this book's organization. Unlike most cookbooks, it lists the recipes in alphabetical order rather than by category. That's because I expect people to use the book when they're hunting for a specific "best," not idly thumbing through the pages trying to decide what to make for dinner.

For the most part, I've alphabetized the recipes by each dish's main quality. Chocolate Cheesecake is with the other cheesecakes. On the other hand, Fried Chicken and Roast Chicken *do* share the same section. Why is this? Because it makes more sense. *Chicken* is the main thing about both recipes, not friedness or roastedness, just as cheesecake is the main thing about Chocolate Cheesecake and just as salad is the main thing about Green Salad, while potatoes are the main thing about Potato Salad.

If you can't bear to hunt down recipes in this way, you can always turn to the Index. Things are conventionally organized there. But I think it's more fun to read a cookbook with all different kinds of recipes jostled together, just as I prefer bookshelves where books like **Betsy, Tacy & Tib** are snuggled between **The Interpretation of Dreams** and **A Field Guide to the Mammals of North America**.

Take the Ann Hodgman Challenge

ARE YOUR RECIPES better than these? I can't believe it. But if you think your potato salad will make me lie down and cry with shame, send in the recipe. Send them all in! (Well, don't bother to send in your chocolate-chip cookie recipe, because you'll never convince me it's better than mine. Your brownie recipe is similarly unnecessary.) If I get enough recipes together, I'll be able to do another cookbook. **Beat This Again!**, maybe.

Then, too, this book is perhaps not as inclusive as it could be, in that it doesn't contain recipes for every food in the world. Try as I might, I couldn't work up much interest in the best way to prepare kale or the best homemade wine. But I probably should have found the best pancake recipe, and I didn't. I should have done more with strawberries, too, and with marinades.

So if you feel you have the best recipe for a food that absolutely must be printed in a second **Beat This!**, mail it to me in care of my publishers. They, in turn, will gently break the news that other people besides me have good recipes. And then I suppose I'll have to be a good sport about it.

Priceless Almond Triangles

THESE STARTED OUT as pecan squares. They were spectacular, but I thought pecans made them too lethal. You don't want people actually *groaning* every time they take a bite. So I decided to use almonds instead. The triangles are even more popular with almonds. I've never brought them anywhere without being asked for the recipe.

Triangles, by the way, always make a bar cookie look more impressive. And, as author and fellow former-Rochesterian Nicholson Baker has pointed out, it's much more fun to bite into something triangular than something rectangular.

Crust
2	cups all-purpose flour
⅔	cup confectioners' sugar
⅛	teaspoon salt
1	cup (2 sticks) unsalted butter, cut into 16 slices
1	teaspoon vanilla extract

Topping
1	cup (2 sticks) unsalted butter
½	cup mild-tasting honey
1 ¼	cups light brown sugar, packed
¼	cup sugar
⅛	teaspoon salt
¼	cup heavy cream
8	ounces slivered almonds
8	ounces unblanched whole almonds, coarsely chopped
1	teaspoon grated orange rind

Crust: Preheat the oven to 350 degrees F.

Place the flour, confectioners' sugar and salt into the bowl of a food processor. Blend for a few seconds. (Keep your hand over the top of the feed tube so the sugar won't fly away.) Then scatter the butter pieces and vanilla on top of the flour mixture. Process with on-and-off pulses until the mixture begins to hold together.

Divide the dough into 8 pieces and space them evenly on an ungreased 10-x-15-inch baking pan. Dipping your fingertips in flour, pat out the dough until it covers the pan evenly.

Bake the crust in the bottom third of the oven for 15 minutes. Then take it out, but leave the oven on. Meanwhile, prepare the topping.

Topping: Place the butter, honey, sugars and salt in a heavy saucepan. Stirring constantly, heat over a medium-low heat until the butter melts and the mixture is well combined. Raise the heat to medium and bring the mixture to a boil. Boil, without stirring, for 1 minute.

Take the saucepan off the heat and stir in the cream, all the almonds and orange rind. Pour this mixture over the bottom crust and stick the pan back in the oven, still in the bottom third of the oven.

Bake the triangles (of course, they're not triangles *yet*) for 20 minutes at 350 degrees. Then turn up the heat to 375 degrees, transfer the pan to the middle of the oven, and bake for another 15 to 20 minutes. The topping should be amber-colored and bubbling all over before you take it out.

Cool the pan on a wire rack. When the topping is completely cool, use a sharp knife to cut it into 20 squares. Lift the squares out of the pan and place them on a cutting board before you cut them into 2 triangles each. Getting triangular bars out of a pan can be an ugly scene.

Store in a tightly covered container.

Makes 40 triangles.

"Pecans make these bars too lethal. You don't want people actually *groaning* every time they take a bite."

Apple Crisp

EVEN AT ITS BEST—like this recipe—apple crisp is just a family food. But I need a regular fix of it all winter long, and this is my favorite way to prepare it.

This recipe is actually even better if you replace the apples with 4 cups of blueberries. The best thing to use, strangely, is frozen, unthawed blueberries. Just pour the little rattlers into your baking dish and take it from there. Because of starting out frozen, they'll end up holding their shapes better than fresh blueberries.

4	cups peeled, sliced cooking apples (I use Granny Smiths)
1	tablespoon plus 1 teaspoon fresh lemon juice
½	cup all-purpose flour
1¼	cups old-fashioned rolled oats
⅔	cup light brown sugar, packed
1¼	teaspoons cinnamon
½	teaspoon salt
¼	teaspoon freshly grated nutmeg
⅛	teaspoon ginger
½	cup (1 stick) unsalted butter, melted

Preheat the oven to 375 degrees F.

Place the apples in a greased 8-inch-square baking dish and toss with the lemon juice. In a medium bowl, combine the flour, rolled oats, brown sugar, cinnamon, salt, nutmeg and ginger. Add the melted butter and mix until crumbly. Pat the mixture on top of the apples. Bake for 30 minutes and serve hot with heavy cream.

Serves 4.

The Best *Regular* (or I Guess I Should Say Classic) Apple Pie

Two crusts. No crumb topping. No rum. No raisins. Remind me why people like apple pie so much? Well, partly because of the cinnamon, or at least that's why I like it. It took a McDonald's apple pie, of all things, to make me realize how important cinnamon is. (I'm saying "of all things" to make it sound as though I never eat at McDonald's.) Their little pillow-shaped pie-let was completely spackled with cinnamon, and it was actually quite good.

In fact, it was good enough to persuade me to forego Sausage Biscuits for breakfast and switch to Baked Apple Pies from then on. (McDonald's has to say Baked so you won't think they're fried.)

This pie has cinnamon in the crust, twice the normal amount of cinnamon in the filling and cinnamon on top. You could even top it with some Cinnamon Ice Cream (page 192), but that would probably be overkill. Vanilla is fine.

Pastry
- 2 ½ cups all-purpose flour
- 2 teaspoons cinnamon
- ¼ teaspoon salt
- 1 cup (2 sticks) unsalted butter, softened
- ¼ cup Crisco
- 5 tablespoons ice water
- 1 teaspoon vanilla extract

(continued)

Filling

3   pounds Granny Smith apples (enough to make 8 cups sliced), peeled,
     cored and thinly sliced
1   tablespoon fresh lemon juice
½   cup sugar
⅓   cup light brown sugar, packed
3   tablespoons cornstarch
2   teaspoons cinnamon
½   teaspoon freshly grated nutmeg
2   tablespoons unsalted butter

    Milk for brushing the top crust
1   tablespoon sugar mixed with ½ teaspoon cinnamon

Pastry: Stir together the dry ingredients. Cut in the butter and Crisco using whatever pie-crust method works best for you. (I use a pastry blender myself.) When the mixture resembles coarse meal, sprinkle in the ice water and the vanilla. Gently gather the dough into a ball with a fork. Divide it into sort-of halves. (One half should be a little bigger than the other half.) Press each "half" into a disk about 1 inch thick. Wrap each in plastic wrap and chill for ½ hour. While they chill, prepare the filling.

Filling and assembly: Preheat the oven to 350 degrees F. (You never need to cook a pie crust at a high temperature. It makes it shrink and overbrowns it.)

Butter the bottom and sides of a 9-inch pie tin. On a floured rolling surface, roll out the smaller "half" of dough until it forms a circle about 12 inches in diameter. Line the pie tin with the dough, being careful not to stretch the dough anywhere. Stick the tin in the refrigerator for 15 minutes.

Put the apples into a medium bowl and toss with the lemon juice. In a separate large bowl, place the dry ingredients and stir to combine. (Unless you're specifically told not to, always combine the fruit with the dry ingredients just before you fill a pie crust. Otherwise the fruit will get too juicy.) Leave the two bowls alone for a while while you get the crust into the oven.

Butter the shiny side of a 14-inch square of aluminum foil. Place the foil, butter-side down, in the pastry-lined pie tin. Fill it with 2 cups of pie weights, raw rice or dried beans. Bake the shell on a cookie sheet for 20 minutes, or until slightly gilded. Transfer to a rack. Remove the pie weights and foil and cool the crust.

As the crust cools slightly, roll out the other disk of dough into a circle about 13 inches in diameter. Let it sit for a sec.

Toss together the apples and the other filling ingredients, except the butter. Working quickly, fill the pie shell with the filling. Sprinkle little hunks of the butter all over the apples. Then top with the top crust and crimp the edges together. (This may be a little tricky. Unbaked pie dough has no reason to stick to baked dough. But it doesn't matter if it doesn't look perfect.) Trim off any ragged edges; a pair of scissors works better than a knife for this. Cut several slits in the shape of ovals in the top crust to let the steam out as the pie bakes; make sure they're big enough not to close up as the crust expands.

Quickly brush the top crust with milk. Lavishly sprinkle the top of the pie with the cinnamon sugar. Bake the pie on the bottom rack of the oven on a cookie sheet for 1 hour. (The cookie sheet helps concentrate heat on the bottom of the pie tin, which in turn helps make the bottom crust flakier.) Then transfer the pie to the middle rack and bake for another 10 minutes.

Cool slightly before cutting.

Now you are an American.

Makes one 9-inch pie.

Pecan-Apple Pie

U NIQUE AND OUT OF THIS WORLD," the original recipe, from a Rochester, New York, Junior League cookbook, promised. The original pie in that original recipe was supposed to be baked with the pecan topping underneath and then unmolded. Sure! Yeah! It's really easy to unmold a hot pie! To increase the dough's tensile strength, there was only a tiny bit of shortening in the crust. Even when you unmolded the pie success-fully, half the pecans would stick in the pan and have to be laboriously re-attached with brown-sugar glue. And the bottom crust (which, of course, became the top crust) never got browned enough.

So I fiddled around a little and produced the following, which is my own particular apple pie of choice. Now the glazed pecans start out on top. The pie doesn't have to be upended, and it looks great. Oh, and tastes great, too.

The all-important raisin step

The night before you make the pie, put ¾ cup golden raisins into a small bowl. Sprinkle them with 2 tablespoons bourbon and let them macerate overnight. Stir them once in a while, if you think of it. Then go to bed.

Next day, make the pastry.

Pastry
- 3 cups all-purpose flour
- ¼ cup confectioners' sugar
- ½ teaspoon salt
- 1¼ cups (2½ sticks) unsalted butter, softened
- ¼ cup Crisco
- ½ cup ice water
- 1 teaspoon vanilla extract

Filling
- 6–8 cups peeled, cored and thinly sliced Granny Smith apples
- 2 tablespoons fresh lemon juice
- ½ cup sugar
- 2 tablespoons cornstarch
- 1 teaspoon cinnamon

½ teaspoon freshly grated nutmeg
¼ teaspoon salt
1 teaspoon grated lemon rind
¼ cup (½ stick) unsalted butter, softened
⅔ cup light brown sugar, packed
¾ cup pecan halves, the smaller the better

Pastry: Stir together the dry ingredients. Cut in the butter and shortening until the mixture resembles coarse meal. Sprinkle in the ice water and vanilla and gently gather the dough into a ball with a fork. Divide the dough into sort-of halves, one a little bigger than the other. Press each "half" into a disk about an inch thick. Wrap each disk in plastic wrap and chill while you prepare the filling.

Filling and assembly: Preheat the oven to 350 degrees F.

Butter the bottom and sides of a 9-inch pie pan (if you used 6 cups of apples) or a 10-inch pie pan (if you used 8 cups). On a floured rolling surface, roll out the smaller round of dough until it forms a circle about 12 inches in diameter. Line the pie pan with the dough, being careful not to stretch the dough anywhere. Stick the pan in the refrigerator for 15 minutes.

Put the apples into a medium bowl and toss with the lemon juice. In a separate large bowl, place the sugar, cornstarch, spices, salt and lemon rind. In a separate small bowl, cream the butter and brown sugar. Let the filling ingredients—and the pecans—rest while you go back to work on the crust.

Butter the shiny side of a 14-inch square of aluminum foil. Place the foil, butter-side down, in the pastry-lined pie pan. Fill it with 2 cups of pie weights, raw rice or dried beans. Bake the shell on a cookie sheet on the bottom rack of the oven for 15 minutes. Leave the cookie sheet in when you take out the pie pan. Transfer the pie crust to a rack. Remove the pie weights and foil and cool the crust.

While the crust cools slightly, roll out a top crust about 13 inches in diameter. If you can, slide it onto a cookie sheet and chill it during the next steps. If not, don't worry. Working quickly, toss together the apples with the dry ingredients and the lemon rind. Drain the bourboned raisins and add to the apples. Fill the bottom crust, fit on the top crust and crimp the two crusts together.

Prick the top of the crust with a fork in several places. (You can't cut holes in it as for regular apple pie, for reasons that will become evident in a minute.)

Carefully spread the top crust with the brown-sugar-butter mixture. Press the

"Sure! Yeah! It's really easy to unmold a hot pie!"

pecans into the butter mixture, covering the entire top crust. It is, of course, nice if you arrange them decoratively.

Bake the pie on the cookie sheet on the bottom rack of the oven for ½ hour. Then move it up to the top third of the oven and bake it for another ½ hour. It may drip a bit, so you'll really need the cookie sheet.

Cool the pie on a rack while you say a prayer of thanks that you don't have to unmold it now.

Makes one 9- or 10-inch pie.

Apricot Conserve

I DON'T MUCH LIKE the taste of cooked vinegar, which pretty much lets out chutneys for me. (Sorry, Mum. The secret is out.) This conserve is what I use instead. Granted, it's sweeter than most chutneys. In fact, I can remember coming home as a teenager to find my younger sister railing, "There are no cookies in this house! There's nothing dessert-y in this house! I had to eat *apricot conserve!*"

Not that it's a good dessert replacement, but isn't it nice to know that you can eat it straight out of the jar the way my sister did? It's also perfect with pork and ham and chicken dishes, and I've even been known to press it into service as a condiment when I make Indian foods. (Sort of a mock chutney, I guess.)

I'm giving you the full recipe because this does, in fact, make a nice thing to give away at Christmastime. But since I don't make it to give away, I always halve the quantity myself.

3	pounds dried apricots
3	pounds golden raisins
3 ½	pounds sugar
3	large oranges, seeded, cut into small pieces and chopped fine—rind and all — in a food processor
3	cups chopped walnuts, lightly toasted

Put the apricots in a large, heavy saucepan, and pour over just enough water to cover them. Bring to a boil, then lower the heat and simmer the apricots until they're tender, about 10 to 15 minutes. Add the raisins, sugar and chopped oranges.

Simmer for ½ hour, stirring. It should be thick enough for you to imagine that you can serve spoonfuls of it without its running all over the plate. (Keep in mind that it will become thicker as it cools.) When the conserve is as thick as you want it, remove it from the heat. Cool the mixture, and stir in the walnuts.

You can seal this in sterilized jars and all that, but I never do. I just put it into a big crock and put the crock in the back of the refrigerator.

Makes 7 quarts.

Artichoke and Mushroom Salad

HERE'S A RECIPE you probably didn't realize you were trying to find the best version of. But how can I not include it when it's so good and I might never get the chance to write another cookbook?

It must be made several hours ahead.

¼	cup red-wine vinegar
¼	cup vegetable oil
2	teaspoons Dijon mustard
1	large clove garlic, minced
2	teaspoons chopped fresh tarragon or ½ teaspoon dried
1	cup half-and-half
1	9-ounce package frozen artichoke hearts, cooked and cooled
2	cups thinly sliced mushrooms
1 ½	cups green beans: trimmed, sliced diagonally into 1-inch lengths and lightly steamed
	Salt and fresh-ground black pepper to taste

In a small bowl, whisk together the vinegar, oil, mustard, garlic and tarragon. Still whisking vigorously, add the half-and-half in a slow, steady stream until the dressing is thoroughly mixed. Let the dressing sit at room temperature for 1 hour to let the flavors meld.

Combine the vegetables in a large bowl. Pour the dressing over them and mix gently but thoroughly. Season with salt and pepper. Chill the salad for at least 2 hours before serving.

Serves 4.

Best Banana Bread

I CAN'T CALL EVERY RECIPE in this book "The Best So-and-So," so from time to time I try to work in a catchy alliterative title. "Beautiful," for instance, but that wouldn't work in this case. All banana bread looks the same. "Blissful Banana Bread" is the kind of thing you'd see in a vegetarian cookbook from the seventies. "Big"? "Buttery"? Yuck—buttered bananas. I tossed various terrible ideas around until I realized that "Best Banana Bread" was alliterative as well as accurate. So I just went with the flow.

2	cups sugar
1	cup (2 sticks) unsalted butter, at room temperature
6	very ripe medium bananas
4	large eggs, well beaten
1	tablespoon fresh lemon juice
2	teaspoons grated orange rind
2½	cups cake flour, sifted
2	teaspoons baking soda
1	teaspoon salt

Preheat the oven to 350 degrees F. Butter two 9-x-5-inch loaf pans.

Cream the sugar and butter until light and whipped-creamy. Add the bananas, eggs, lemon juice and orange rind; beat until uniformly blended. It may take a while to get rid of the banana lumps.

Sift together the dry ingredients and fold lightly but thoroughly into the banana mixture. Pour the batter into the prepared pans. Bake for 45 to 55 minutes, until the loaves are firm in the middle and the edges begin to pull away from the pans.

Cool the loaves on racks for ½ hour before you remove them from the pans.

Makes 2 loaves. This bread freezes very well.

Barbecue Sauce

I'M SOMETHING OF AN EXPERT on barbecue sauce, having once been a judge at a barbecue contest in Ohio. I thought I was pretty lucky, but then it turned out that one of my fellow judges, in addition to being a barbecue judge, had an actual paying career testing the amusements at amusement parks.

At the contest I ate 42 ribs in 24 hours. I tried ribs with sauce that tasted like crayons, ribs with sauce that tasted like ketchup, ribs with sauce that tasted like corn syrup. There were also some ribs with sauce that tasted like great barbecue sauce. But since I already knew that the best barbecue sauces were to be found in Kansas City, my heart wasn't in my work. Only my stomach was.

Kansas Citians argue constantly about barbecue sauce. As an outsider (it's only my hometown-*in-law*, not my hometown), it's easy for me to step in and settle the dispute. There are two best barbecue sauces. One is from Arthur Bryant's Barbecue Restaurant, and one is from Gates Bar-B-Q.

Although my husband and I buy both sauces by the case, the two are very different. Bryant's is thin, acrid and grainy—in a nice way, of course. Gates's sauce is thicker and sweeter, more like what most people think of as barbecue sauce. But it makes supermarket sauces taste like melted Popsicles.

There's no point in making your own barbecue sauce when the pros do it so much better. Call these guys and get them to send you some. The number at Bryant's is (816) 231-1123. The number at Gates is (816) 923-0900.

Beef Stew

I'M MORTIFIED to present you with a recipe based on canned soup. But not mortified enough *not* to present the recipe. This is a better stew than any I've made on top of the stove. I've tried dolling it up by replacing the soup with canned plum tomatoes, and it wasn't nearly as good. You have to use the soup. At least it's not cream of mushroom.

I'm not yet a big expert on cuts of meat. But I don't use the meat that's cut up and sold as stew beef. It's usually too fatty and gristly. Instead I buy whatever large chunk of beef looks okay to cut up for stew that day: bottom round, London broil, even tenderloin once in a while. (Well, I don't *buy* tenderloin for stew. I use it if I have a few odds and ends of it in the freezer.)

2	pounds suitable-for-stew beef, cut into cubes
6	carrots, cut in thick slices
2	large onions, chopped coarsely
1	large baking potato, cut into big "stew-size" dice
1	bay leaf
1	teaspoon dried oregano
1	teaspoon salt
½	teaspoon fresh-ground black pepper
1	can Campbell's Tomato Bisque soup
½	soup can water, dry red wine or beer

Preheat the oven to 275 degrees F. In a lidded casserole, combine the beef, carrots, onions, potato and bay leaf. Sprinkle the seasonings over all and mix well. In a small bowl, combine the soup with whichever liquid you choose and pour it over the stew ingredients. Cover the casserole first with a tight layer of foil and then with the lid.

Bake the stew for 5 hours. After the first 2 hours, check it every ½ hour or so to make sure there's enough liquid. There probably will be, but it's no fun to take the lid off when the 5 hours are up and be presented with a scorched mess.

There's certainly no reason you can't dress this recipe up a little if you want to. Thick-sliced mushrooms would be a nice addition, for example, as would a handful of chopped parsley added at the end. But don't knock yourself out. This is stew you're making, not beef bourguignon.

Serves 6.

Beef Tenderloin

I AM INDEBTED to Helen Hecht's wonderful **Simple Pleasures** for this method. As she explains in that book, the low oven temperature produces evenly cooked meat that's uniformly rare, "rather than having a wide band of well-done meat surrounding a bloody center." Hecht also says that if you wish to serve the beef cold, you should wait to slice it until just before serving. Otherwise it will go brown on you. (She said it more elegantly, of course.)

1   **4-5 pound beef tenderloin, tied and trimmed, at room temperature**
1   **clove garlic, sliced in half**
   Lots of fresh-ground black pepper

Preheat the oven to 500 degrees F.

Rub the tenderloin all over with the cut garlic. Then rub it liberally all over with the pepper. (Save salt for after the meat is cooked. Salt draws out meat juices during cooking.) While you're doing this, take note of how thick the meat is.

Place the meat in a roasting pan, stab a meat thermometer into its heart and place the pan in the oven. Immediately turn the heat down to 225 degrees. If you've decided you have a thin tenderloin, start checking the temperature on the meat thermometer after ½ hour; if you have a normal-sized tenderloin, start checking after 50 or 60 minutes. The thermometer should read 140 degrees for rare meat.

When the meat is done, let it stand for 10 minutes before you cut it. Don't forget to put salt on the table.

Serves 8 to 10.

Baking-Powder Biscuits

THE MAIN THING I look for in a baking-powder biscuit is lightness. At one point I thought I'd have to switch to making yeast-raised biscuits to get them as light as I wanted, but then I decided that the flour was more important than the leavening. (I was right.) Which is really just as well, because it somehow seems cheaty to use yeast in a baking-powder biscuit— like adding helium to a bread recipe.

2	cups cake flour
4	teaspoons baking powder
1	teaspoon sugar
½	teaspoon salt
½	teaspoon cream of tartar
½	cup (1 stick) unsalted butter, chilled and cut into 8 slices
½	cup milk and ½ cup heavy cream, combined in the same measuring cup

Preheat the oven to 400 degrees F. Lightly butter a 9-x-13-inch baking pan.

In a food processor, blend the cake flour, baking powder, sugar, salt and cream of tartar. (Put your hand over the feed tube, or a great cloud of flour will float into the air.) Add the butter and pulse the mixture on and off until it resembles fine bread-crumbs.

Transfer the dry-ingredient mixture to a bowl and stir in enough of the milk-cream mixture to produce a soft dough. (You'll need at least ⅔ to ¾ cup liquid.) Turn the dough out onto a floured surface and knead it gently for a few seconds.

Roll the dough out with a rolling pin on a lightly floured surface to a thickness of ½ inch. (Any thicker and the biscuits may topple over in the oven.) Then cut out biscuits with a 2-inch cutter and place them on the prepared baking pan with their sides just touching. They don't fill the whole pan, so I always make a fake pan side of aluminum foil to put against the "open edge" of biscuits. This helps them hold their shape.

Bake the biscuits for 20 minutes, or until lightly browned. Let them cool in the pan for a couple of minutes before removing them.

Makes 8 two-inch biscuits.

Jim Paisley's Current Black Bean Soup

I DON'T MEAN Jim puts *currants* in it. I mean it's the one he currently makes, unlike the spaghetti sauce he used to make (see page 174) that he wrongly thinks I stole from him, even though our recipes for it are *completely* different.

1	pound dried black beans, chilled for 24 hours in water to cover
2	tablespoons corn oil
4	carrots, coarsely chopped
3	medium onions, coarsely chopped
6	cloves garlic, minced
2	tablespoons minced fresh jalapeño pepper
1	tablespoon ground cumin
2	smoked ham hocks
3	cups chicken stock
1	cup dry sherry
	Juice from 1 lime
	Sour cream and chopped fresh cilantro for garnish

Rinse the beans and drain them in a colander while you start the vegetables.

Heat the oil in a large, heavy soup-related pot and sauté the carrots, onions and garlic until they are softened but not browned—about 5 minutes. Stir in the jalapeño and cumin and cook for a couple minutes more.

To the vegetables, add the drained black beans, ham hocks, chicken stock and enough water to cover.

"Now here's the part that's a lie," says Jim. "The recipe says cook for 2 hours, but you have to cook it for 4 hours. They want you to eat more soup, so they always underreport the cooking time by 100 percent."

Anyway, cook the soup over low heat, stirring frequently, for 4 hours, or until the beans are tender. Remove the ham hocks. Stir in the sherry and the lime juice and serve immediately with sour cream and chopped cilantro.

Serves 6.

Bleu Cheese Dressing

REALLY GOOD BLEU CHEESE dressing isn't that thick, pasty stuff you find in salad bars. It's a sharply flavored vinaigrette with discrete bits of bleu cheese throughout. The best way to make a good bleu cheese dressing is *not* to combine the cheese and the vinaigrette ahead of time. Rather, prepare each separately, then toss them together in the salad. Does that still count as dressing? I hope so.

- 4 tablespoons corn oil
- 2 tablespoons balsamic vinegar
- 1 tablespoon Dijon mustard
- 1 small clove garlic, minced
  Fresh-ground black pepper to taste
- 3 ounces bleu cheese, or to taste

Whisk together the oil, vinegar, mustard, garlic and pepper until emulsified. Do not add salt.

Crumble the bleu cheese into small pieces.

First toss the salad greens with the vinaigrette and then—carefully—with the bleu cheese. With a dressing this assertive, endive, watercress and radicchio make a nice combination of greens.

Makes about ⅔ cup dressing.

Sugar Hill Blueberry Muffins

THAT THESE ARE THE BEST of their kind isn't a matter of opinion, but simple fact. Not only are they the best, but they're also the toughest. They freeze beautifully; they refrigerate beautifully; they can sit out on the counter all day without withering. I graciously acknowledge your thanks in advance. (Actually, your thanks are due to the Sugar Hill Inn in Franconia, New Hampshire.)

You will notice, in this book, a reliance on frozen blueberries. That's because they hold their shape better when cooked. The time it takes them to thaw is the time that fresh blueberries would be cooking.

This recipe works well with other fruits too. Chopped peaches combined with toasted almonds are a particularly fortuitous mix.

1	cup all-purpose flour
1	teaspoon baking powder
½	teaspoon baking soda
½	teaspoon salt
2	large eggs
1	cup sour cream
5	tablespoons unsalted butter
1	cup light brown sugar, packed
1	cup old-fashioned rolled oats
1	cup frozen or fresh blueberries (if frozen, do not defrost)
2	tablespoons sugar

Preheat the oven to 375 degrees F.

Line a 12-cup muffin tin with muffin-cup liners. This recipe does not work without them. Combine the flour, baking powder, baking soda and salt in a small bowl. Set aside.

In a large bowl, beat the eggs with the sour cream until thoroughly combined.

In a medium saucepan, over medium heat, melt together the butter and the brown sugar. Beat this mixture into the egg mixture. Stir in the oats.

Fold in the flour mixture and then the blueberries. Fill the muffin cups two-thirds full. Drop a generous pinch of sugar onto the top of each muffin.

Bake the muffins for 25 to 28 minutes. Cool for 5 minutes, then remove muffins (in their papers) and finish cooling them on a rack.

Makes 1 dozen.

Blueberry Ice Cream

THERE'S A BLUEBERRY-PICKING PLACE not far from my house where the blueberries are the size of grapes and so unblemished that I don't want to know what they're sprayed with. So I never ask. I just pick.

I can't think of anything funny to say about something as purple and velvety as this ice cream, but I'll keep trying. Like so many of the other things I eat, this is adapted from a Helen Hecht recipe. (No, no, that wasn't trying to be funny.)

1	dry pint fresh blueberries (2 ½ cups), washed and picked over
¾	cup sugar
¼	cup fresh lemon juice
1	cup heavy cream
½	cup half-and-half
6	large egg yolks, well beaten
1	teaspoon vanilla extract

In a heavy saucepan, over medium-low heat, place the blueberries, sugar and lemon juice. Bring the mixture to a boil, stirring frequently. Let it continue to boil slowly for 35 minutes. Cool the mixture and puree it in a food processor or blender.

Scald the heavy cream and half-and-half together. Lower the heat to very low. Put a little jolt of hot cream into the egg yolks and stir it in quickly. Pour the yolk-cream mixture into the hot cream/half-and-half mixture, whisking constantly. Cook the yolk-cream mixture over low heat, stirring, until it thickens and coats the back of a spoon, or until it reaches 170 to 180 degrees F. Put the pan holding the custard into a larger pan of ice water and stir the custard frequently until it is cool, about 20 minutes.

Combine the blueberry puree and the custard. Chill overnight. The next morning, give the mix a few good stirs and freeze it in an ice-cream machine according to the manufacturer's directions. Transfer the ice cream to a sealed container and freeze.

Makes 1 quart.

Blueberry Pie

THE FIRST THING you have to do is make sure you have 1½ cups of frozen blueberries waiting in the freezer. (You will be using them to remind your guests that what they are eating is a pie with blueberries in it, not a pie made of blueberry jam.) Either use the frozen blueberries that come unsweetened in bags, or freeze some of the fresh ones you are also going to be using in this pie.

Pastry
2½ cups all-purpose flour
½ teaspoon cinnamon
¼ teaspoon salt
 Pinch freshly grated nutmeg
1 cup (2 sticks) unsalted butter, softened
¼ cup Crisco
5 tablespoons ice water
1 teaspoon vanilla extract

Filling
3½ cups fresh blueberries, washed and picked over
1 cup sugar
2 tablespoons cornstarch
¼ teaspoon salt
⅛ teaspoon freshly grated nutmeg
3 tablespoons butter, melted
1 tablespoon fresh lemon juice
1½ cups frozen blueberries (keep them frozen until the minute you need them)
 Confectioners' sugar for dusting the top

Pastry: Preheat the oven to 350 degrees F.

In a large bowl, stir together the flour, cinnamon, salt and nutmeg. Cut in the butter and Crisco, using whatever pie-crust method works best for you. When the mixture resembles coarse meal, sprinkle in the ice water and the vanilla. Gently gather the dough into a ball with a fork. Divide it into halves. Press each half into a disk about 1 inch thick. Wrap each disk in plastic wrap and chill for ½ hour.

While they chill, start getting the filling ready.

33

Filling and assembly: Pour the fresh blueberries into a medium bowl. In a small bowl, combine the sugar, cornstarch, salt and nutmeg. In another bowl, combine the melted butter and lemon juice. Keep the mixture warm, maybe on top of the preheating stove.

Butter the bottom and sides of a 9-inch pie tin. On a floured rolling surface, roll out one disk of dough until it forms a circle about 12 inches in diameter. Line the pie pan with the dough, being careful not to stretch the dough. Stick the pan in the refrigerator for 15 minutes.

Butter the shiny side of a 14-inch square of aluminum foil. Place the foil, butter-side down, in the pastry-lined pie tin. Fill it with 2 cups of pie weights, raw rice or dried beans. Bake the shell on a cookie sheet for 20 minutes, or until it is slightly gilded. Transfer to a rack, remove the pie weights and foil and cool the crust.

As it cools slightly, roll out the other dough disk into a circle about 13 inches in diameter. If you want to make a lattice top, cut the rolled-out dough into 14 strips about ¾ inch wide. (If you've never made a lattice top and would like to, you can learn how to do it by reading another cookbook. Otherwise just leave it in a circle.)

Working at dizzying speed, toss together the fresh blueberries and the combined dry ingredients. Sprinkle in the melted butter and lemon juice mixture and toss the ingredients together. Then scatter the frozen blueberries over the other ingredients and toss again.

Pour the filling into the pie shell. Then weave a lattice crust or fit the plain old regular top crust on. Crimp the edges of the two crusts together and use scissors to trim off any raggedy bits. If you haven't made a lattice, cut several slits in the shape of ovals in the top crust to let steam out.

Bake the pie on the bottom rack of the oven, on a cookie sheet, for 1 hour. (The cookie sheet helps concentrate heat on the bottom of the pie tin, which in turn helps make the bottom crust flakier.) Then transfer it to the middle rack and bake for another 10 minutes.

As soon as the pie is out of the oven, dust the top lightly with sieved confectioners' sugar.

Cool the pie slightly before cutting. Serve with vanilla ice cream.

Makes one 9-inch pie.

"You will notice a reliance on frozen blueberries. That's because they hold their shape better when cooked."

Best Bran Muffins

I UNDERTOOK to find the best bran muffin more as a public service than anything else. I'm not a big bran-muffin fan. I'd eat a bran muffin if I were starving, but if I were in a muffin store I'd buy a different kind. If I had to eat one, though, it would be made from this recipe.

Then I might even have seconds.

3	cups bran cereal (100% Bran, for example)
1¼	cups dark raisins
⅔	cup corn oil
1	cup boiling water
2	cups buttermilk
⅓	cup molasses
¼	cup honey
2	large eggs, well beaten
1	teaspoon grated orange rind
2¼	cups all-purpose flour
¼	cup light brown sugar, packed
2½	teaspoons baking soda
½	teaspoon salt

Into a large bowl, dump the bran cereal, the raisins and the corn oil. Pour the boiling water over them and stir well. Let the mixture cool a bit.

In another bowl, combine the buttermilk, molasses, honey, eggs and orange rind. Pour the resulting liquid into the cereal mixture and stir well.

Combine the flour, brown sugar, baking soda and salt in yet another bowl. Add them to the cereal mixture. Stir just to combine; then cover the bowl and let it stand for 1 hour.

Preheat the oven to 400 degrees F. Line 24 muffin cups with muffin-cup liners. Fill the cups three-fourths full of batter.

Bake the muffins for 20 to 25 minutes. Cool in the tins for a few minutes. Then gingerly lift them out and let them finish cooling on a rack.

Makes 2 dozen muffins.

The Coach House Bread-and-Butter Pudding

COMFORT in its most sublime form.

12	small, thin slices of French bread
	Unsalted butter for buttering the bread
5	large eggs
4	large egg yolks
1	cup sugar
⅛	teaspoon salt
4	cups milk
1	cup heavy cream
1	teaspoon vanilla extract
¼	cup confectioners' sugar for dusting the top
1	12-ounce bag of frozen, unsweetened raspberries

Preheat the oven to 375 degrees F.

Butter each slice of bread on one side. (The original recipe says to cut off the crusts, but I can't stand to.)

Beat together the eggs, egg yolks, sugar and salt until thoroughly blended. Combine the milk and cream in a saucepan and scald them. Stir slowly into the egg mixture; add the vanilla extract. Strain the custard.

Butter a 2-quart baking dish and line it with the bread, which should be placed buttered-side up. Pour the strained custard over the bread.

Into a large roasting pan, put about 1 inch of hot water. Place the baking dish in the roasting pan, making sure the sides of the baking dish do not touch the sides of the roasting pan. Bake the pudding for 45 minutes, or until it tests done.

Sprinkle the confectioners' sugar all over the top of the pudding and pop the baking dish quickly under the broiler until the sugar forms a glaze.

Serve the pudding hot or cold, with raspberry sauce that you've made by thawing those raspberries and forcing them through a fine sieve along with their juice.

Serves 6 to 8.

Brownies

WHEN YOU think about it, "brownie" is not a very helpful word. What's great about brownies is not, after all, their brownness. It's probably too late to change the name to "frosting you can pick up"—but that quality is what makes *these* brownies the best. They're so creamy and unctuous that you could spread them on top of other brownies if you wanted to. What's the point of cakelike brownies, anyway?

You can get away with using store-brand semisweet chocolate in these brownies, but they're far better with any of the Lindt, Tobler or Callebaut semisweet chocolates. I use Callebaut for the unsweetened chocolate. I order it in 5-kilo blocks from a supply house called Maid of Scandinavia, which is worth doing simply so you can be on their mailing list. (Haven't you ever wanted to know where to go for praying-hands decorations to put on the tops of your cakes?)

These must be made at least 6 hours ahead of serving time.

1   cup sugar
2   large eggs at room temperature (you can soak them in lukewarm water
     for ½ hour to take the chill off)
     Pinch salt
5   ounces best-quality semisweet chocolate
3   ounces best-quality unsweetened chocolate
½   cup (1 stick) unsalted butter
¼   cup all-purpose flour
1   teaspoon vanilla extract
1   cup miniature chocolate chips

Preheat the oven to 375 degrees F. Butter an 8-inch-square pan.

In a large bowl, beat the sugar, eggs and salt for 15 minutes. This is much easier if you own a stand-up mixer and can roam around the kitchen straightening up while the mixture beats. If all you've got is a hand mixer, however, plan on having a book in your other hand. Just check the bowl once in a while to make sure the egg mixture isn't migrating out onto your counter.

Meanwhile, melt the semisweet and unsweetened chocolates and butter in a double boiler over a very low flame. When the mixture is about three-quarters melted, take it off the heat and stir until the chocolates and butter are completely melted and the mixture is smooth. Cool to lukewarm (don't rush this!) and fold gently into the sugar-egg mixture. Fold in the flour, vanilla extract and finally the chocolate chips.

Spread the mixture in the prepared pan and set it in the middle of the oven. Bake for 20 minutes if you like your brownies custardy the way I do. (If you like them a little drier, then bake them for 30 minutes. They'll still be nice and creamy.) Cool on a rack for 6 hours and cut into squares.

Makes one 8-inch-square pan.

Layered Brownies

ONE OF my oldest friends gave my family this recipe when I was little. She was little too, of course. It puts all other layered brownies to shame, with their skimpy little unbrowned butter. Growing up, my siblings and I called these Stupid Brownies—the idea being, I guess, that the layering made them look stupid. I've since revised my thinking.

Brownies
- ½   cup (1 stick) unsalted butter
- 6   ounces unsweetened chocolate
- 2   cups sugar
- 4   large eggs
- ⅛   teaspoon salt
- 1   cup all-purpose flour
- 1   teaspoon vanilla extract

Frosting
- ½   cup (1 stick) unsalted butter
- 2   cups confectioners' sugar
- ¼   cup heavy cream
- 2   teaspoons vanilla extract

Glaze
- 4   ounces unsweetened chocolate
- 3   tablespoons unsalted butter

Brownies: Preheat the oven to 300 degrees F. Butter a 9-x-13-inch pan and line it with buttered parchment paper cut to fit the bottom of the pan.

In small pan, over very low heat, or in a double boiler, melt the butter and chocolate. While the mixture cools, beat together the sugar, eggs and salt for 8 minutes. Fold in the chocolate mixture, then the flour and vanilla. Pour the batter into the prepared pan and bake for 30 minutes, or just until the mixture pulls away from the sides of the pan. Cool thoroughly.

Frosting: Melt the butter over low heat until it is a definite caramel in color. Remove it from the heat. Immediately beat in the confectioners' sugar, heavy cream and vanilla. Frost the brownies with this mixture while it is still warm. Cool to room temperature.

Glaze: In a small pan over very low heat, or in a double boiler, melt together the unsweetened chocolate and the butter. Pour this glaze over the top of the white icing. (The best way to do this is to pour the chocolate on and tilt the pan back and forth until covered.)

When the glaze has hardened—it will take an hour or two—cut the brownies into squares. (It is easier to do this neatly while the brownies are still at room temperature.) Then chill the brownies thoroughly. They're much better eaten cold.

Makes one 9-by-13-inch pan.

The Best Homemade Bubble Stuff

OKAY, it's not food, but neither is play-dough. And the corn syrup does provide quick energy to your lawn when your children spill this on their way to the backyard.

Mix together in a dishpan:

6	cups water
2	cups Crystal Octagon dishwashing liquid
¾	cup light corn syrup

Now take it out and give it to the kids. They should use it right away.

"The corn syrup does provide quick energy to your lawn."

Buttercrunch

BUTTERCRUNCH is a very basic candy, but it's tremendously popular. Master this recipe, and you control the world. You'll need a candy thermometer. Of course, you need one all the time. This is my first chance to mention how useful a candy thermometer is, and I'm not going to let you off the hook until you own one. Until you do, there will always be some dessert you want to make but can't, all because you wouldn't buy a little strip of metal.

This is, I think, the only recipe in which I use salted butter. I've tried making the candy with unsalted butter and adding salt, but for some reason it wasn't as good. So every Christmas I go out and buy ten pounds of salted butter just for making buttercrunch.

1   **cup (2 sticks) lightly salted butter**
1   **cup plus 2 tablespoons superfine sugar**
1   **tablespoon light corn syrup, dissolved in 2 tablespoons warm water**
8   **ounces slivered almonds, lightly toasted and chopped fine, and divided in half**
6   **ounces semisweet chocolate**

Grease a large, heavy saucepan and in it melt the butter over medium-low heat. As soon as it's melted, stir in the sugar. Continue to stir constantly until the sugar has dissolved and the mixture comes to a rolling boil. Add the corn syrup-water mixture and stir well; the mixture will hiss and spit for a few seconds, but that's all right.

With the pan still on the heat, cover the saucepan and leave it covered for 3 minutes. Then uncover it and stick in the candy thermometer. Keeping the heat at medium-low, and stirring once in a while, heat the mixture to 300 degrees F. At some point before it reaches that temperature (say when it's 220 degrees, where it will seem to stay forever), scatter half the toasted almonds evenly over the bottom of a 9-x-13-inch baking pan.

When the candy reaches 300 degrees, remove it from the heat immediately and pour it into the almonded pan, tilting the pan back and forth to cover it evenly. (Wear oven mitts. The pan gets incredibly hot.) *Do not scrape the saucepan*, or the candy might crystallize. Let cool.

When the candy is cool, heat the semisweet chocolate in the top of a double boiler until it's about two-thirds melted. Take the chocolate off the heat and stir until the remaining chocolate is melted as well.

Pour the chocolate onto the cooled candy and spread it over the candy's entire surface with a rubber spatula. Sprinkle the rest of the almonds over the chocolate.

Cool the candy until the chocolate is set, about 2 hours or longer. Turn the pan upside down on a surface covered with wax paper. Rap the bottom of the pan until the sheet of buttercrunch comes out. Then break the buttercrunch into bite-sized pieces. (Some of the almonds will fall off, but it doesn't matter. That's why you put on more than you needed.)

Buttercrunch keeps well (I'm not going to make that hoary old joke about "as long as you manage to hide it") and freezes well. Unlike many candy recipes, this one can be multiplied and made exactly the same way. If you go the whole hog and multiply it by 5 and make lots and lots of batches and give away dozens of boxes of buttercrunch every year—as I do—make sure to put the candy into plastic bags before you box it. Otherwise, grease stains will gradually make their way through to the surface of the boxes, which wouldn't be very Christmas-y.

Makes about 1 pound.

"This is my first chance to mention how useful a candy thermometer is, and I'm not going to let you off the hook until you own one."

Porter's Butterscotch Sauce

PORTER PERHAM is one of my family's oldest friends. He's a wonderful cook and the first person who ever served my family spinach noodles. I was about eight, and I thought they were wildly exotic.

Try this sauce on coffee ice cream with salted, toasted pecans on top.

½ **cup (1 stick) unsalted butter**
1 **pound light brown sugar, packed**
1 **cup heavy cream**
Dash salt (that's what Porter calls it, a "dash")
1 **teaspoon vanilla extract**

Melt the butter and brown sugar together over low heat, stirring until the butter is melted and the sugar is dissolved and everything is nice, about 5 to 10 minutes. Stir in the heavy cream and the salt and mix well. Transfer the sauce to a double boiler and cook it over simmering water for 1 hour. Stir in the vanilla, and there you go.

Makes 2 ½ cups.

Pure, Rich, Great Caramels

WHEN we moved from New York to a small town in Connecticut, the house we bought had an apartment on the third floor. In that apartment was, naturally, a kitchen. Something about country life suggested candymaking to me (perhaps it was the fact that I wasn't able to *get* candy as easily as I had in the city), and once I learned that in Connecticut you could sell food you'd made only if you were equipped with a second, non-family kitchen. . . well, then it just seemed as though I was *meant* to be a candymaker.

I wasn't, though. The candy was fine, but when my husband discovered that each box I sold was costing me $60, I began to think that I was in the wrong line of business. I returned to the slightly more lucrative field of freelance writing, but I kept my recipes (along with thousands and thousands of gold foil labels and candy boxes and frilled paper cups and dipping forks).

I still make these caramels as often as I can. They're beyond perfect. I *beg* you to make them at least once in your lifetime. Buy a trashy novel, pull the kitchen stool up to the stove and start stirring.

Oh, and find your candy thermometer.

2	cups sugar
1	cup light corn syrup
¼	teaspoon salt
2	cups heavy cream
¾	cup evaporated milk
½	ounce unsweetened chocolate
1½	teaspoons vanilla extract

Lightly oil the bottom and sides of a large, heavy saucepan. In the saucepan, combine the sugar, corn syrup, salt and 1 cup of the heavy cream.

Stirring constantly, bring the mixture to a boil. As soon as it boils, slowly add the remaining 1 cup of cream. Keep stirring, stirring, stirring until the mixture's temperature is 232 degrees F, about 1 hour. Now slowly add the evaporated milk, trying not to make the mixture stop boiling. (But don't worry if it does. Eventually the temperature will begin to climb again.)

Drop in the chocolate and stir it around. Now settle in for a really long period of stirring, at least 1 hour. The candy has so few degrees to go, and yet it takes so long!

When the thermometer at last creeps up to 242 degrees, take the candy off the heat. Stir in the vanilla—don't worry if the mixture bubbles and hisses for a few seconds—and then pour the candy into an ungreased 8-x-8-inch pan. *Do not scrape the saucepan.* No matter how steadily you stir, there still may be little bits of scorched stuff on the bottom of the pan, and you don't want to scrape them into the candy. Also, it's a good idea never to scrape any saucepans in which you've made candy (unless you're just scraping up the leftovers into your mouth). Doing so might make the candy crystallize.

Cool the sheet of caramel to room temperature. I said an ungreased pan because if you grease it, it will make the candy too greasy. Now, however, you'll have to trick the caramel into coming out of the pan. The best way to do this is to stick the pan into the freezer for several hours.

Then cover your kitchen counter with plastic wrap. Place the pan upside down on the plastic wrap and pound it very hard with your fists or a hammer. The caramel should drop right out. If it doesn't come out the first time, refreeze for ½ hour and try again.

Now you have to let the caramel come back to room temperature. When it does, use kitchen scissors to cut that big, luscious sheet into 1-inch pieces. Keep them on the plastic wrap, or you'll never get them off your counter. Or at least I've never heard of anyone freezing a counter.

Wrap the pieces in wax paper, more plastic wrap or candy wrappers, which you can find in specialty shops and at Maid of Scandinavia (see page 208).

Makes about 1½ pounds.

"I beg you to make these at least once in your lifetime. Buy a trashy novel, pull the stool up to the stove and start stirring."

Carrot Cake

Tₕɪꜱ ɪꜱ another recipe I wish were my own. Alas, it's not. It's from a very worthwhile book called **The Frog/Commissary Cookbook**. The cake itself is delicious; the pecan filling is sublime. As far as I'm concerned, the only good confectioners'-sugar icing is a cream cheese one.

I've made one change from the original recipe. It called for raisins to be added to the cake batter and coconut to the icing. That seemed excessive to me, considering everything else that's going on with this cake, so I deleted them. Feel free to reinsert them, though.

You'll need to make the pecan filling 1 day ahead.

Pecan Cream Filling
- 1 ½   cups sugar
- ¼   cup all-purpose flour
- ¾   teaspoon salt
- 1 ½   cups heavy cream
- ¾   cup (1 ½ sticks) unsalted butter
- 1 ¼   cups chopped pecans, lightly toasted
- 2   teaspoons vanilla extract

Carrot Cake
- 1 ¼   cups corn oil
- 2   cups sugar (preferably superfine)
- 2   cups all-purpose flour
- 2   teaspoons cinnamon
- 2   teaspoons baking powder
- 1   teaspoon baking soda
- 1   teaspoon salt
- 4   large eggs
- 4   cups grated carrots (about 1 pound)
- 1   cup chopped pecans

(continued)

47

Icing

1	cup (2 sticks) unsalted butter, at room temperature
8	ounces cream cheese, at room temperature
1	1-pound box confectioners' sugar
1	teaspoon vanilla extract
	Pinch salt

Pecan Cream Filling: A day before you make the cake, blend the sugar, flour and salt in a heavy saucepan. Gradually stir in the cream. Add the butter. Cook and stir the mixture over low heat until the butter has melted; then let simmer 20 to 30 minutes until golden brown, stirring occasionally. Cool to lukewarm. Stir in the pecans and vanilla. Let the mixture cool completely. Refrigerate it overnight. If it is too thick to spread, bring it to room temperature before using.

Carrot Cake: Preheat the oven to 350 degrees F. Generously butter and flour a 10-inch tube pan.

In a large bowl, whisk together the corn oil and the sugar. In another bowl, sift together the flour, cinnamon, baking powder, baking soda and salt. Sift half the dry ingredients into the oil-sugar mixture, then blend well. Sift in the rest of the dry ingredients while adding the eggs, one at a time. Mix well. Add the carrots and pecans and mix again.

Pour the batter into the prepared tube pan. Bake for 70 minutes, or until the cake begins to pull away from the sides of the pan. Cool upright, in the pan, on a cooling rack. While the cake is baking, prepare the icing.

Icing: Cream together the butter and cream cheese until well blended and fluffy. Sift in the confectioners' sugar. Cream again. Then beat in the vanilla and the salt. If the icing is too soft to spread, chill it for a few minutes. Refrigerate it if you don't plan to use it right away, but bring it back to room temperature before using.

Assembling the cake: Run a spatula around the inside of the tube pan to loosen the cake. Invert the cake onto a serving plate. With a long serrated knife, carefully split the cake into 3 horizontal layers. Spread the pecan filling between the layers. (You may not need it all.) Frost the top and sides of the cake.

If you want, decorate the top of the cake in the time-honored fashion: Reserve ½ cup of the icing. Color half of it orange and half green. Through a ⅟₁₆-inch icing tube, pipe little orange carrots; then pipe green tops for them. Don't worry if the carrots don't taper enough. People will get the point.

Serves 12.

"As far as I'm concerned, the only good confectioners'-sugar icing is a cream cheese one."

Carrots With Ginger and Cumin

THIS WOULD come under the category of Best Unexpected Thing To Do With Carrots, not Healthiest Way To Use Carrots. But I'm sure you have plenty of healthy carrot recipes.

You can make this dish ahead and reheat it if you want to. Purees thrive on that treatment.

1	pound carrots
2	teaspoons ground cumin
6	tablespoons unsalted butter
1	tablespoon peeled, chopped fresh ginger
2	cloves garlic, chopped
2	tablespoons fresh lemon juice
½	cup milk
	Salt and fresh-ground black pepper

Scrape the carrots and cut them into medium slices. Cook them in a vegetable steamer until they are just tender. Shock them under cold water to stop the cooking.

Sauté the cumin in 1 tablespoon of the butter for about 30 seconds. Add the ginger and garlic and sauté 1 minute longer.

Combine the drained carrots with the cumin-garlic mixture, lemon juice, remaining butter and milk. Process this mixture until smooth. (There will still be some bits of carrot throughout to give the puree a bit of texture.)

Season the puree to taste. Serve immediately or refrigerate and reheat the next day.

Serves 4.

Cheese Straws

THESE NEVER seem to go out of style. Once I made a huge batch of them for a big party, and people kept asking if they could take the leftovers home.

Making cheese straws is kind of a procedure, though. Don't start when your son is also using the kitchen to make his science project and your spouse is whistlingly unloading the dishwasher. Otherwise you will become tight-lipped and nasty. Give yourself plenty of time and elbow room. I usually make cheese straws when everyone else in the house has gone to bed.

1   batch Puff Pastry (page 168)
8   ounces Parmesan, plus more if needed

Prepare a batch of Puff Pastry. After final chilling, roll out the pastry to an oblong 18 x 6 inches. Cut the oblong in half and chill both halves while you prepare the cheese.

In a food processor, "grate" as fine as possible the Parmesan cheese. Spread half the grated cheese on the surface on which you'll be rolling the pastry. (I find it easiest to cover my counter first with plastic wrap and roll the cheese straws directly on the counter. When it's time to clean up, it's simple just to gather up the plastic wrap.)

Take one of the pastry halves out of the refrigerator and place directly onto the "cheesed" surface. Roll out into a rectangle about ⅛ inch thick, turning the dough a couple of times so that all of it is well coated with cheese. (The object is actually to roll the cheese into the dough.) When the dough is well coated with cheese on both sides, return it to the refrigerator and repeat the process with the other half of the dough and the remaining cheese. (If for some reason you run out of grated cheese, grate some more.)

Cover two cookie sheets with parchment paper. Cut the dough into strips ½ inch wide and whatever length you want. It's not important that the straws all be the same length. Some of them are going to break in two anyway. Place them close together on the cookie sheet (they will expand up, not out). When both cookie sheets are filled, chill the straws again while you preheat the oven to 375 degrees F.

Bake *one sheet at a time* for 12 to 15 minutes, or until well browned and cooked through. You may need to break one open to see. Allow to cool thoroughly on the parchment before removing very, very carefully. If you are baking further batches, make sure the cookie sheets are thoroughly cooled before reusing. These can be frozen unbaked and baked directly from the freezer; they'll take about 10 minutes longer.

Store in a tightly sealed container.

Makes about 40 eight-inch cheese straws.

Mom-Style Cheesecake

THIS IS THE CHEESECAKE I was raised on, and it's still the kind I like best. Originally the recipe came not from my own Mom-style Mom but from a friend of hers, Sue Olson. When I make the recipe nowadays, I follow all of Sue's directions except that I make her sour cream "icing" twice as thick. (Immoderation in all things, as my father never says.)

I also prepare the cake's crust from homemade graham crackers. I do realize that this sounds as though I make my own lettuce for salads. I may not be able to persuade you to make your own graham crackers—although it's very easy, and they do taste better, and you should be ashamed of yourself if you don't try them—but at least I hope I can steer you away from those boxes of premade crumbs. Or, worse, those premade crusts. They taste exactly like sweetened pencil shavings.

Graham Crackers
- 1 ⅓   cups whole-wheat flour
- 1   cup all-purpose flour
- ½   cup light brown sugar, packed
- ¾   teaspoon baking soda
- ½   teaspoon salt
- ½   teaspoon cinnamon
- ¼   teaspoon ginger
- ¼   cup (½ stick) unsalted butter, cut into slices
- ⅓   cup honey
- 5   tablespoons cold water
- 1   teaspoon vanilla extract

Crust
- 1 ¼   cups graham cracker crumbs
- 3   tablespoons butter, melted
- 2   tablespoons sugar

Filling
- 1   pound Philadelphia Cream Cheese, at room temperature
- 4   large eggs, separated
-    Pinch salt
- ¾   cup sugar
- 1   teaspoon vanilla extract

Topping

2   **cups sour cream**
2   **teaspoons sugar**
1   **teaspoon vanilla extract**

Graham Crackers: Preheat the oven to 325 degrees F.

Place the flours, brown sugar, baking soda, salt, spices and butter in the bowl of a food processor. Combine with a few on-off pulses and add the remaining ingredients. Pulse a few more times, then process for 30 seconds, or until the mixture forms a ball.

Divide the dough in half and cover half with plastic wrap. Butter a rimless cookie sheet. (We don't have to be too precise about the size because you're not actually going to make nice, neat, square graham crackers. You're going to make a big sheet of graham cracker that you can turn into crumbs.) Dust the dough with flour and roll it out until it covers the entire baking sheet. Prick the dough all over with a fork.

Now repeat the process with another baking sheet and the rest of the dough. (If you did want to make actual graham crackers, by the way, you'd cut the sheets of dough into squares and lightly score the squares down the middle with a knife before pricking them with the fork.) Bake both these massive crackers for 15 minutes, or until brown and firm to the touch. Lift them off with a spatula—it doesn't matter if they break—and cool them on racks.

At last, you're ready to start your cheesecake. First produce 1¼ cup of crumbs from your graham crackers by crushing them with a rolling pin or grinding them in a food processor.

Crust: Preheat the oven to 350 degrees F. Combine the crumbs, the butter and the sugar until well blended. Butter the bottom of a 9-inch springform pan and press the crumbs over it. Bake the crust for 10 minutes.

While it bakes, you can start the "cheese" part of your cheesecake.

Filling: Cream the cream cheese with the egg yolks and salt until light. Beat in the sugar until the mixture is light. Beat in the vanilla. In a separate bowl, beat the egg whites until stiff and fold them gently but thoroughly into the cheese mixture.

Pour the batter into the baked crust and bake for 28 minutes exactly. (When you take it out, it will still be quivery, but it will firm as it cools.) While the cheesecake bakes, make the topping.

"Immoderation in all things, as my father never says."

Topping: Stir together the sour cream, sugar and vanilla. Let it rest until you need it.

Remove the cheesecake from the oven—*without* turning off the oven—and cool it for 10 minutes. Turn the oven off, and cool the cheesecake for another 5 minutes. Spread the sour-cream icing over the top of the cheesecake. Put the cake back into the turned-off but still-cooling oven, and let it stand for 7 minutes.

Now take the cake out of the oven for good. Cool it to room temperature and chill thoroughly. Remove the sides of the springform pan just before serving.

Makes one 9-inch cheesecake.

New New-York-Style Cheesecake

As FAR AS I can make out, "New York" cheesecake usually means "stiff, heavy and floury." This version gives the city its due.

Crust
- ⅔ cup all-purpose flour
- 1 tablespoon sugar
- 1 teaspoon grated lemon rind
- Pinch salt
- ⅓ cup (5 ⅓ tablespoons) unsalted butter, cut into 6 slices

Filling
- 2 ½ pounds Philadelphia Cream Cheese, at room temperature
- 1 ⅓ cups sugar
- 1 tablespoon all-purpose flour
- Grated rind and juice from 2 lemons
- 6 large eggs
- ¼ cup heavy cream
- ¼ cup sour cream
- Pinch salt
- 1 tcaspoon vanilla cxtract

Crust: Preheat the oven to 350 degrees F. Butter the bottom and sides of a 9-inch springform pan.

Into the bowl of a food processor, place the flour, sugar, lemon rind and salt. Combine them with a few on/off pulses. Scatter the slices of butter over the dry ingredients, then process until the mixture forms a dough.

Divide the dough into 4 pieces that are roughly the same size; space the balls of dough at even intervals on the bottom of the prepared pan; and pat the dough until it covers the bottom of the pan in an even layer. Pierce the dough with a fork in several places. Bake for 20 minutes, or until the crust is golden brown. Cool the pan on a rack while you prepare the cheese part of the cheesecake.

Turn the oven down to 275 degrees.

Filling: In a large bowl, cream together the cream cheese and sugar until light. Beat in the flour, lemon rind and lemon juice. Then add the eggs, one at a time, and beat until the mixture is smooth. Beat in the heavy cream, sour cream, salt and vanilla. Pour the mixture into the prepared pan.

Bake the cheesecake for 2½ hours. (The middle of the cake will still be a little quivery, but it will set as it cools.)

Turn the oven off, open the oven door, and let the cheesecake cool inside the open oven for ½ hour. Then cool the cheesecake to room temperature on a cake rack. Chill thoroughly before serving.

This cake screams to be served alongside a pile of fresh strawberries.

Makes one 9-inch cheesecake—12 servings.

Chocolate Cheesecake

Is chocolate cheesecake still an issue? Or has it gone the way of chocolate mousse? To me it seems to be faintly dusted with Sixties powder. ("Chocolate cheesecake? Oh, yes, you'll find it between the Metrecal and the onion dip.") But *I* like chocolate cheesecake, and I've never had any complaints from the people I've served it to. Besides, this is *my* book.

Well, enough ranting. I think chocolate cheesecake is best with a crumb crust rather than a pastry crust. The crust should be made with chocolate wafer cookies, and you *should* make your own. But I'm not looking over your shoulder.

These chocolate wafers are from **Maida Heatter's Book of Great Chocolate Desserts**. The cheesecake is based on one that appears in **Maida Heatter's Best Dessert Book Ever**. I added the topping all by myself. Maida Heatter didn't tell me to do it. But I would have if she had.

Chocolate Wafers for the Crust
- 2 ounces unsweetened chocolate
- 1 cup plus 2 tablespoons sifted all-purpose flour
- ¾ teaspoon baking powder
- ¼ teaspoon baking soda
- Pinch salt
- ¼ cup (½ stick) unsalted butter, softened
- ½ cup sugar
- 1 teaspoon vanilla extract
- 1 large egg
- 1½ teaspoons milk

The Crust Itself
- 1 cup chocolate wafer crumbs
- ⅓ cup sliced almonds, lightly toasted
- 2 tablespoons sugar
- ¼ cup (½ stick) unsalted butter, melted and cooled

(continued)

Filling

1	pound semisweet chocolate, chopped fine
1½	cups heavy cream
3	tablespoons Dutch-process cocoa powder
1½	tablespoons instant espresso or coffee powder
¼	teaspoon salt
1	tablespoon dark rum
4	large eggs
2	pounds (four 8-ounce packages) Philadelphia Cream Cheese, at room temperature
1	cup sugar
1	teaspoon vanilla extract

Topping

4	ounces semisweet chocolate
1	cup sour cream
	Pinch salt

Chocolate wafers: Partially melt the chocolate in a double boiler. Remove the double boiler from the heat when the chocolate is halfway melted; stir the chocolate until it's completely melted and smooth.

Sift together the flour, baking powder, baking soda and salt.

In the large bowl of an electric mixer, cream the butter. Add the sugar and vanilla and beat well. Add the melted chocolate and beat until it's all blended in. Then add the egg and the milk and beat well once more. On low speed, add the sifted dry ingredients, scraping the bowl with a rubber scraper and beating only until incorporated.

Place the dough on a piece of wax paper. Cover it with another piece of wax paper and press down with your hands until the dough is about 1 inch thick. Scrumple the edges of the paper up to wrap the dough. Chill the dough for 20 minutes.

Adjust two oven racks to divide the oven into thirds. Preheat the oven to 400 degrees F. Cover two large cookie sheets with parchment paper.

On a lightly floured pastry cloth, with a floured rolling pin, roll out the dough until it is a teensy ⅛ inch thick. Cut it into slabs and transfer the sheets of rolled-out dough to the cookie sheets. It doesn't matter how big the sheets are so long as they are thin.

Bake two sheets at a time for 7 to 8 minutes. After 4 minutes, reverse the sheets top to bottom and front to back; this ensures even baking. Bake until the large, formless "cookies" feel firm to the touch. Cool them on racks.

For the crust, crush enough baked wafers to produce 1 cup of crumbs with a rolling pin or grind them up in a food processor. If you're going on with the cheesecake at this point, lower the oven heat to 350 degrees and butter the bottom of a 9- or 10-inch springform pan.

Actual crust: In a food processor, finely grind the chocolate wafer crumbs, almonds and sugar. Add them to the melted butter in a small bowl and stir until everything is blended. Press the crumb mixture into the bottom of the prepared springform pan. Bake for 10 minutes.

Now lower the oven to 275 degrees and go on to the filling.

Filling: Over low heat, half-melt the chocolate in a double boiler. When it's half-melted, remove the double boiler from the heat and stir until the chocolate is all melted and smooth. Set it aside uncovered.

In a small saucepan, over moderate heat, scald ½ cup of the cream. When you see a wrinkled skin on top, sieve in the cocoa and stir in the espresso or coffee powder and salt. Whisk until smooth. Then cook for a few minutes, stirring constantly. Remove the saucepan from the heat and stir in the rum and the remaining 1 cup cream. Set this aside uncovered too.

Beat the eggs well in a small bowl. In the large bowl of your electric mixer, beat the cream cheese until it is completely, completely smooth. It can't have any lumps. (White lumps of cream cheese would look—well—grublike in chocolate cheese-cake.) Maida Heatter suggests, "It is best to remove the beaters once during mixing, scrape them clean with a fingertip, then replace them and continue beating." That doesn't work quite as well if you have an electric mixer with a balloon whisk instead of beaters, but carry on.

Add the sugar and vanilla and beat, scraping down the sides of the bowl frequently, until the mixture is perfectly smooth. Then add the chocolate. The minute it's incorporated, add the cream mixture; the minute it's incorporated, add the beaten eggs. After you've added the eggs, beat the batter as little as possible. The last thing you want is an airy cheesecake.

Pour and scrape the mixture into the prepared springform pan. It will come almost to the top. Smooth it with a spatula if you need to.

> "I like chocolate cheesecake, and I've never had any complaints. Besides, this is my book."

Bake the cheesecake for 2 hours. Then turn off the heat and let the cake stand in the oven with the door open for ½ hour. After that, cool it on a cake rack.

When the cake has thoroughly cooled, make the topping.

Topping: Melt the chocolate in a double boiler. Stir in the sour cream. Quickly spread the topping over the cake.

Chill the cake before serving. Remove the sides of the springform pan just before serving.

Makes 1 very rich 9- or 10-inch cheesecake—12 to 16 servings.

Chicken Betty's Fried Chicken

I DON'T WANT TO SOUND LIKE **The Bad For You Cookbook** here. I'm not telling you that you *have* to use lard. I'm just saying it makes the best fried chicken. Same with the MSG. No one is *making* you use it! But as long as you're using lard, for God's sake, you might as well use the MSG too.

Chicken
3-3 ½	pounds chicken, cut in serving pieces, rinsed and thoroughly dried with paper towels
1	large egg
1	cup milk
	Approximately 2 cups all-purpose flour
2-3	tablespoons fresh-ground black pepper (not teaspoons)
1	cup lard
1	cup solid vegetable shortening
1	tablespoon salt
1	teaspoon monosodium glutamate (available in the spice section of the supermarket as Ac'cent)

Gravy
2	tablespoons all-purpose flour
1 ½	cups milk, scalded
	Salt and fresh-ground black pepper

Chicken: Remove the chicken from the refrigerator ½ hour before you start the recipe, to coax it along toward room temperature.

Beat the egg with the milk in a wide, shallow bowl. Set next to it a plate covered with wax paper for seasoning the chicken. Put the flour into a 9-x-13-inch baking pan and stir in 1 tablespoon of the pepper.

Combine the lard and the shortening in a 12-inch cast-iron skillet and melt them over low heat. The combined fats, when melted, should be 1 inch deep. If necessary, adjust the fats to achieve the correct depth, being sure to keep the same proportion of lard and shortening.

Dip each piece of chicken into the egg mixture, covering both sides. Then place each piece on the wax-paper-covered plate and season liberally, on both sides, with the remaining pepper, salt and MSG.

Put the seasoned chicken, one piece at a time, into the pan of peppered flour. Turn the chicken over and over in the flour—pressing down hard—until it is thoroughly coated. Tap the floured chicken pieces against one another gently to remove excess flour. Turn up the heat and heat the fats until hot. (A piece of bread, dropped into the pan, will sizzle.) Place the chicken pieces in the hot fat; do not crowd.

Fry the chicken over medium-high heat for 7 minutes on each side, or until browned. Then cover the pan three-fourths of the way, reduce heat to medium-low and fry the chicken for 15 to 18 minutes longer. Turn the chicken frequently, making sure it is not browning too fast. (If necessary, lower the heat.) Add more lard and shortening if necessary.

Drain the chicken on a stack of paper towels. Some of the smaller pieces may cook faster than the rest; they can be kept warm in the oven, in a baking pan, at 250 degrees F.

Gravy: For gravy (which is served on biscuits or mashed potatoes, not on the chicken), empty the fat from the pan, but leave the browned flour in the pan. Heat the pan over low heat until the browned flour begins to simmer.

Stir in the 2 tablespoons flour. Whisk constantly over low heat, for 5 to 8 minutes, or until the flour browns and combines with the drippings to form a thick paste. Pour in the hot milk, whisking constantly until smooth and thick. Add salt and pepper to taste. (You practically *can't* put in too much pepper.) Simmer the gravy for 7 or 8 minutes more, stirring, adding more milk as necessary to achieve a heavy-creamish consistency. Season to taste, making sure there really is plenty of pepper.

Serves 4.

"I'm not telling you that you *have* to use lard. I'm just saying it makes the best fried chicken."

A Completely Different Fried Chicken

BUT maybe even better.

- ¾ cup fresh lime juice
- ¼ cup soy sauce
- 3 tablespoons dark rum
- 2 tablespoons minced garlic
- 1 tablespoon grated fresh ginger
- 3½ pounds chicken, cut into pieces
- 2 cups corn oil
- 2 cups all-purpose flour
- Lime wedges

Mix the lime juice, soy, rum, garlic and ginger in a large ceramic or stainless-steel bowl.

Marinate the chicken in this mixture, in the refrigerator, for 24 hours. Bring the chicken to room temperature before frying it.

Heat the corn oil to 375 degrees F. Drain the chicken and shake it around in a brown paper bag filled with the flour. Fry the chicken in the hot oil, a few pieces at a time, for about 10 minutes on each side, or until golden brown.

Drain the chicken on paper towels. Serve it with the lime wedges.

Serves 5 to 6.

Perfect Roast Chicken

PERFECT, that is, if you like crisp garlicky skin, moist flesh with a hint of lemon and pan juices you have to force yourself not to drink straight from the pan.

1	3-pound chicken
2-3	thin-skinned lemons (they will be smoother and shinier—and juicier—than the thick-skinned variety)
1	large clove garlic
1	tablespoon coarse (Kosher) salt
1	cup water

Preheat the oven to 400 degrees F. Remove the giblets and any excess fat from the cavity of the chicken.

Roll the lemons to soften them. Then pierce each lemon with a skewer in about 20 places. Peel the garlic and put it through a garlic press.

In a small bowl, mash the garlic together with the salt. When you have a nice odorous paste, smear half of it inside the chicken's cavity. Then put in the lemons. (You may not be able to fit all 3 of them.) I always truss the chicken at this point, but you don't absolutely have to.

Rub the rest of the salt-garlic paste all over the outside of the chicken. Then put the chicken on a rack and put the rack in a roasting pan. Pour the water into the bottom of the pan.

Bake the chicken for 1 hour, or until the drumstick just begins to move in the socket. You don't need to baste it. In fact, you shouldn't. Nor should you remove the lemons from the chicken's cavity when serving; they're not very pretty at this point. But you should definitely serve the chicken with the pan juices.

Serves 4.

Chicken Salad for Company

THIS SALAD—from Suzanne's restaurant in Washington, D.C.—is divinely inspired. I've never met anyone who didn't love this recipe, but perhaps it made me happiest when an itinerant preacher visited my church one evening and we gave him a potluck supper. He said he had never tasted anything like this salad, and asked if he could take some to eat on his travels the following day. I liked to think of him eating it under a tree somewhere. (Hey, maybe the recipe really is divinely inspired.)

3	whole chicken breasts, poached according to the method on page 67 and cut into bite-sized pieces
1	large sweet red pepper, cut into julienne strips
2	large heads broccoli, cut into florets
12	slices thick-cut bacon, cooked crisp and crumbled
¾	cup sour cream
¾	cup mayonnaise
4½	tablespoons Dijon mustard
4½	tablespoons raspberry vinegar
2	tablespoons finely chopped fresh dill

Combine the chicken with the red peppers in a large bowl.

In a vegetable steamer, steam the broccoli for 2 to 3 minutes, or until it just starts to get tender. Add it to the chicken and mix it in gently. Mix in the crumbled bacon.

Whisk together the sour cream, mayonnaise, Dijon mustard, raspberry vinegar and dill. Pour the dressing over the chicken and vegetables and mix well. Chill the salad for at least 2 hours before serving.

Serves 4 to 6.

Mom-Style Chicken Salad

WHAT DOES MOM-STYLE MEAN when it comes to chicken salad? I polled a bunch of friends and got a bunch of answers. "Plain mayonnaise for the dressing," said one person, "or that gross white salad dressing." "Grapes," another told me firmly. "Seedless grapes, cut in half." "Pasty and white," said a third. Hey! No personal remarks about Mom, please!

I guess that what people were trying to tell me was that a homey chicken salad is soothing, dull and mayonnaise-y. You know: *chicken salad.* Something suitable for 50 women at a luncheon party. Something you could serve inside a cantaloupe without hurting either the salad's or the cantaloupe's feelings. The following recipe is more challenging than that. It's not even white, but pale-green; it's certainly not bland. This is Helen Hecht's basic recipe. I changed the lettuce to broccoli.

3	whole chicken breasts, split and poached(see page 67)
¼	cup fresh parsley sprigs, packed
3	scallions, cut into 1-inch pieces
1	small clove garlic, peeled
2	tablespoons white-wine vinegar
1	teaspoon Worcestershire sauce
¾	cup mayonnaise
⅔	cup sour cream
2	cups cooked broccoli, separated into florets
	Salt and fresh-ground black pepper
	Fresh watercress for garnish

Remove the skin from the chicken breasts; remove the meat from the bones. Cut the chicken into strips (a serrated knife works well for this).

In a food processor or blender, mince the parsley, scallions and garlic with the vinegar and Worcestershire sauce. Add the mayonnaise and process until smooth. Turn the dressing into a small bowl and fold in the sour cream.

Two hours before serving, combine the chicken and dressing and refrigerate. Stir in the broccoli just before you serve the salad. Season to taste with salt and pepper. Garnish the bowl or platter with fresh watercress.

Serves 6.

Carol's Perfect Poached Chicken-Salad Chicken

YOU NEED boneless chicken breasts for this, as many as—well, as you need. Let them come to room temperature. Bring a large pot of water to a rolling boil. With tongs, place the chicken in the water and remove it the instant the water stops boiling. Turn the same water up to a full boil again. Put the chicken back in, turn the heat off, and leave the pot on the stove, covered, for at least 1 hour.

I don't know why this works, but it does. I must mention, however, that it doesn't get the chicken hot enough to kill the Salmonella bacteria. So if you happen to be a worrywart, you might try a more conventional method. I don't plan to change to another method myself; I just want to make you aware of your options.

The Chiliest Chili

PROCLAIMING that your chili recipe is the best is the opposite of shooting fish in a barrel. "What do you mean?" my husband asked when I mentioned this to him. "Having a fish put you into a shooting barrel?" No, no! I mean, you have to sit there cringingly waiting while lots and lots of people (the "fish," you see) take shots at you. People get upset when their chili recipes are challenged.

But let's not let all this fish talk spoil our appetites. When I decided to come up with my own chili recipe, I proceeded on the assumption that *every* chili recipe was the best ever. So I combined them all.

Chili is further proof of my rule that every recipe is better if you add sausage or bacon. Most good chili recipes combine sausage and ground beef. Mine combines sausage and cubed pork. I think the pork—an innovation of my husband's—picks up the flavors better. My husband also suggested putting in salsa, which he uses in *his* chili. "It takes care of a lot of problems," he said mysteriously.

You can use almost any kind of dried beans you want in chili. I use little pink beans, first soaking them, in water to cover, in a covered pot in the refrigerator for twenty-four hours. (This is supposed to make them less, you know, *beany*.) Once, for my husband's birthday, I got him a mail-order package of lots and lots of kinds of dried beans. The cutest were rice beans, which actually did look like grains of rice. If I can get used to the idea of little white things in my chili, I want to try them next.

2	tablespoons corn oil
2	large onions, chopped
1	large red bell pepper, seeded and chopped
3	fresh jalapeño peppers, seeded and chopped fine
1	tablespoon minced garlic
4	tablespoons chili powder
2	tablespoons ground cumin
2	tablespoons snipped fresh dill
1	tablespoon dried basil
1	tablespoon dried oregano

1 tablespoon mild paprika
1 teaspoon fresh-ground black pepper
2 pounds fresh pork, cut into very small pieces
1 pound hot Italian sausage, removed from casings
1 pound sweet Italian sausage, removed from casings
1 cup dried beans of your choice, soaked (see previous page), drained, cooked in water to cover until tender, rinsed and drained again
1 35-ounce can tomatoes and their juice (or one 28-ounce can plus one 15-ounce can)
½ cup "hot" salsa (add more to taste)
¼ cup gold tequila
1 cup beer
3 tablespoons tomato paste
Salt to taste
Sour cream, grated extra-sharp Cheddar and chopped onions as accompaniments

In a large pot, over medium heat, heat the oil. Add the onions and cook until softened but not brown. Add the bell pepper, jalapeños and garlic and cook until the peppers are slightly softened. Do not let the garlic brown.

Stir in the seasonings and herbs and cook for a minute or so longer.

In a large skillet, over medium-high heat, cook the pork and sausage, breaking up the sausage with your spoon as you stir. Cook until the sausage is well browned, the pork has a few crispy bits, and there's no pink meat to be seen.

Drain the skillet well. With a slotted spoon, add the meats to the onion pot.

Over medium heat, stir in the cooked beans, tomatoes, salsa, tequila, beer and tomato paste. Salt to taste. Turn the heat down to low and simmer the chili uncovered, stirring frequently, for 1 hour. (If it gets too thick, you can add water from time to time.) Serve the chili very hot with its various accompaniments.

Serves 6 to 8.

"Chili is further proof of my rule that every recipe is better if you add sausage or bacon."

Best-Named Chocolate Cake (Gallbladder Cake)

THIS RECIPE was contributed by my friend Lisa Meltzer, whose grandfather was a doctor. A note on Lisa's recipe says, "Grandma called it Gallbladder Cake because she always made an eggnog for Papa to use when he did gallbladder X-rays." (According to my dad, who's also a doctor, giving the patient a fatty drink would increase the symptoms of an inflamed gallbladder, or, as he put it, "elicit the symptoms of acute chole-cystitis and help establish the diagnosis." He just said that right out.) The note goes on, "Sometimes he didn't need the eggnog, so she would make a chocolate cake out of it!"

Gallbladder Cake is plain but pleasant, worth having around if you, like me, enjoy chocolate for breakfast but don't want to start off your day too heavily.

2	large eggs
	Milk
1	cup sugar
1	cup all-purpose flour
2	teaspoons baking powder
2	ounces unsweetened chocolate
¼	cup (½ stick) unsalted butter
1	teaspoon vanilla extract

Butter and flour an 8-inch-square baking tin. Preheat the oven to 350 degrees F.

Place the eggs into an 8-ounce (1-cup) measuring cup. Fill the rest of the cup up with milk to the 1-cup line. Pour the eggy milk into a large bowl and beat. Then beat in the sugar. Sift together the flour and baking powder and fold it into the eggnog mixture.

Melt the chocolate and butter in a double boiler over very low heat. Cool slightly, then fold it into the cake batter with the vanilla.

Pour the batter into the prepared pan and bake for 35 to 40 minutes. That's it. You can frost it (when it's cool, of course) or just eat it plain. But you didn't need me to tell you that.

Makes one 8-inch-square cake.

Flourless Chocolate Cake (Lora Brody's Bête Noire)

Lora Brody and I met at a pie contest in New York City. We were similarly horrified by the winning pie, which once again reminded me that Lora has impeccable taste in desserts. I had known this before, of course, because of this recipe.

I can still remember discovering the recipe for this cake in **Growing Up on the Chocolate Diet**. I rushed into the kitchen and started making it right away. Unfortunately, my infant daughter was taking a nap, and when I started to grind up the chocolate in my Cuisinart, she started to scream. It was the first time a noise had ever woken her; we lived in New York City at the time. The cake turned out to be worth it.

½	**cup water**
1 ⅓	**cups sugar**
8	**ounces unsweetened chocolate, chopped fine**
4	**ounces semisweet chocolate, chopped fine**
1	**cup (2 sticks) unsalted butter, cut into small pieces and brought to room temperature**
5	**extra-large eggs, at room temperature (or 6 large eggs)**
	Whipped cream for topping

Preheat the oven to 350 degrees F. Butter a 9-inch round cake pan and line it with a round of parchment paper cut to fit.

In a heavy saucepan, combine the water with 1 cup of the sugar. Bring the mixture to a boil over high heat. Boil it for 4 minutes, or until a candy thermometer reads 220 degrees F.

Take the pan off the heat and immediately add the chocolate pieces, stirring until they are melted and smooth. If the mixture stiffens, don't worry; it will loosen up again when you add the butter. And the butter immediately, bit by bit, stirring until all of it is used.

Place the eggs and the remaining ⅓ cup sugar in the bowl of an electric mixer. Beat on high speed for 15 minutes. If you want to prevent splattering, drape a dish towel over the mixer and bowl.

When the 15 minutes are up, turn the mixer down to low. Add the chocolate mixture, stirring only until it is fully incorporated. Do not overbeat, or air bubbles will form.

Spoon and scrape the mixture into the prepared cake pan. Set the pan in a slightly larger baking pan and pour boiling water around it. Do not allow the sides of the pans to touch.

Place the cake in the oven and bake it for 25 minutes. Insert the sharp point of a knife into the center of the cake; if it comes out clean, the cake is done. If it does not come out clean, continue baking for up to 10 minutes. Don't bake the cake for longer than 35 minutes.

Remove the pan from the water bath and immediately unmold it onto a cookie sheet. Remove the parchment paper. Invert a serving plate over the cake and turn it right side up onto the serving plate. Serve warm, cold or at room temperature. Whipped cream is mandatory.

Serves 6 to 8.

"When I started to grind up the chocolate in my Cuisinart, my infant daughter started to scream."

Mom-Style Chocolate Cake

THIS CAKE is straight out of a Norman Rockwell painting, but it tastes even better than . . . uh . . . than paint and canvas, I guess. Even for a nice traditional cake, the best mixing method can be found in Rose Levy Beranbaum's **Cake Bible**, which is such a good book that I think the Gideons should put it in hotel rooms instead of the regular Bible. But enough of that. Rose Beranbaum's innovation was to beat the dry ingredients together rather than just sifting them, then to add the butter, and last of all to add the eggs and other liquids. (I'm not explaining it nearly well enough.) You can adapt most cake recipes to her method and thereby greatly improve their texture. In fact, her method is so easy that it hardly makes sense not to use it.

This cake already has a nice texture, though. And it *is* a Mom-style cake. Mom doesn't fuss around with new methods. She likes the old ones just fine.

5	ounces unsweetened chocolate
1¼	cups buttermilk
1	cup sugar
1	large egg, separated, plus 2 large eggs, separated (you'll need the whites)
½	cup (1 stick) butter, softened
1	cup light brown sugar, packed
2	cups sifted cake flour
1	teaspoon baking soda
½	teaspoon salt
1½	teaspoons vanilla extract

Preheat the oven to 350 degrees F. Butter two 9-inch cake pans and line them with rounds of parchment paper cut to fit. Butter the parchment paper, then flour the pans.

In a small saucepan, over very low heat, melt the chocolate. When it's melted, add ½ cup of the buttermilk and whisk until the mixture is smooth. Now whisk in the sugar and the 1 egg yolk. Still over low heat, and stirring constantly, cook the mixture for 3 minutes, or until smooth and thick. Now it's a custard. Cool it to room temperature.

Thoroughly cream together the butter and brown sugar. Beat in the remaining 2 egg yolks, one at a time. Resift the cake flour with the baking soda and salt. Add the dry ingredients to the creamed ingredients in three parts, alternating with the remaining ¾ cup of buttermilk; you should begin and end with the dry ingredients.

Stir the cooled custard and the vanilla into the batter.

Beat the 3 egg whites until they are stiff but not dry. Take about a quarter of the beaten whites and stir them into the batter; then carefully fold in the rest. Pour the mixture into the prepared cake pans. If you have Magi-Cake Strips (see page 204), attach them now.

Bake the layers for 25 minutes, or until the cake just begins to leave the sides of the pan. Cool the layers completely on cake racks before you even think about taking them out of the pan. Frost with Mom's Chocolate Frosting.

Makes one 9-inch 2-layer cake.

This cake is at its best the day it's made. If you have to make it ahead for some reason, freeze the layers in plastic wrap. Defrost and frost them on the day you need them.

Mom's Chocolate Frosting

Mom doesn't take a lot of time whipping up fancy buttercreams, either. She probably makes a confectioners'-sugar frosting and has done with it. But she really should know about *this* frosting, which gives far better results and is even easier to make than the one she now uses.

The original of this recipe calls for all semisweet chocolate. That tastes too sour to me, though. I like a bitter-chocolate taste, but not a sour one. Using half milk chocolate tempers the sourness a bit without taking away too much depth of flavor.

Most grocery stores sell 3-ounce bars of imported chocolate in the candy section. Lindt is my preference, but Tobler is also very good.

6	ounces best-quality semisweet chocolate, chopped
6	ounces best-quality milk chocolate, chopped
2	cups (1 pint) sour cream
2	teaspoons vanilla extract
⅛	teaspoon salt

In a double boiler, over low heat, melt the two kinds of chocolate. When the chocolate is three-quarters melted, remove it from the heat and stir until it's all melted. Whisk in the sour cream, vanilla and salt until the mixture is smooth and frosting-y. Frost the cake layers while the frosting is still warm.

This amount will fill and frost two layers, amply if not generously. If you want to make a lot of peaks and swirls, you should increase the recipe by half. You'll have some extra frosting, but I'm sure you can find a use for it. If you have very young children, for example, they'll get a big thrill out of frosting their own vanilla wafers to make tiny little cakes.

Chocolate Cookies

CHOCOLATE SLIDERS, my husband calls these, because of the way they kind of melt down your throat. There can't be any cookies more chocolaty and creamy and adjective-y than these. The woman who tested this recipe said that this is the most chocolate you can put into a cookie and still have it be legal.

4	ounces unsweetened chocolate, chopped
9	ounces semisweet chocolate, chopped
½	cup (1 stick) unsalted butter, sliced into 8 pieces
½	cup all-purpose flour
½	teaspoon baking powder
½	teaspoon salt
4	large eggs
1 ½	cups sugar
1 ½	tablespoons instant espresso powder
2	teaspoons vanilla extract
9	ounces semisweet chocolate chips (preferably a premium brand, such as Guittard)

In a metal bowl set over a saucepan of barely simmering water, melt the unsweetened chocolate, the chopped semisweet chocolate and the butter. When the mixture is two-thirds melted, remove the bowl from the heat and stir until the contents are completely melted. (This is a good thing to do whenever you melt chocolate, which should never be combined with other ingredients when it's too hot.)

Stir together the flour, the baking powder and the salt in a small bowl. In a large bowl, beat the eggs and sugar for 10 minutes at high speed; then add the espresso powder and the vanilla and beat for 2 more minutes. Fold the chocolate mixture into the egg mixture. Then fold in the flour mixture. Then fold in the chocolate chips.

Allow the batter to rest in the refrigerator for 20 minutes while you preheat the oven to 350 degrees F and line some cookie sheets with parchment paper. Then drop heaping tablespoons of the batter onto the cookie sheets, about 2 inches apart.

Bake the cookies, one sheet at a time, for 8 to 10 minutes. Do not overbake. The cookies should be puffed, shiny and cracked on top. Let them cool for a few minutes—so they won't fall apart—and then transfer them to racks to finish cooling. Store airtight. As with many high-intensity cookies, I prefer to serve these chilled.

Makes 3 dozen.

The Only Chocolate Chip Cookies

A COUPLE OF YEARS AGO, my aunt Gail showed me a copy of a letter she'd received in the mail:

> My daughter and I had finished a salad at the Neiman-Marcus Cafe in Dallas and decided to have a small dessert. Because our family members are such "Cookie Monsters," we decided to try the Neiman-Marcus Cookie. It was so good that I asked if they would give me the recipe. She said with a frown, "I'm afraid not." "Well," I said, "Would you let me buy the recipe?" With a cute smile, she agreed. I asked how much, and she responded "Two Fifty." I said with approval, "Just add it to my tab."
>
> Thirty days later I received my statement from Neiman-Marcus. The bottom of the statement said "Cookie Recipe—$250.00." I asked them to take back the recipe and reduce my bill, but they said they were sorry, the bill would stand.
>
> I told her that I was going to see that every cookie lover in the country would have the $250 recipe for nothing. So here it is.

At about the same time, a friend sent me a copy of a letter with almost the same story. Only the name of the company (it was now Mrs. Fields) had changed. (Also, strangely, the woman involved was now "a member of the American Bar Association.")

I don't know which account is true. Maybe neither is. The recipe in the letters is the same, though, and it's definitely the best chocolate-chip cookie recipe in history. I myself would *cheerfully* have paid 250 bucks for it.

5   **cups old-fashioned rolled oats**
8   **ounces semisweet chocolate**
1   **pound (4 sticks) unsalted butter, softened**
2   **cups sugar**
2   **cups light brown sugar, packed**

(continued)

4   large eggs
2   teaspoons vanilla extract
4   cups all-purpose flour
2   teaspoons baking powder
2   teaspoons baking soda
1   teaspoon salt
24 ounces chocolate chips, the largest and best-quality possible ("Maxi" chips are available in some markets; also, see my note under Chocolate, page 205.)

Preheat the oven to 375 degrees F. Line four large cookie sheets with parchment paper.

In a food processor, grind the oats until they turn into a fine powder. (You can also do this in a blender, working in small batches.) Coarsely chop the chocolate and add to the oats, processing until the pieces, too, become as fine as possible. This may take a long time, but the finer the mixture becomes, the better the cookies will be. Set the oat-chocolate mixture aside.

Cream the butter and sugars together in a large bowl. Add the eggs and vanilla and mix well. In another bowl, combine the flour, baking powder, baking soda and salt. Then gradually beat the flour mixture into the butter mixture.

If you're using a heavy-duty standing mixer, add the oat mixture and beat it in. If you're using a hand-held or lightweight mixer, work the oat mixture in with your hands. Mix thoroughly.

No matter what kind of mixer you have, do the next step with your hands. Your fingernails will get very dirty, but there's really no other choice unless you want to wear plastic gloves. Work the chocolate chips into the dough.

(The original recipe calls for 3 cups of chopped nuts to be added at this point. Yuck! Nuts in chocolate-chip cookies. Save them for oatmeal cookies, *I* say.)

"I myself would *cheerfully* have paid 250 bucks for this recipe."

Set the four cookie sheets in front of you. You're about to set up an assembly line. What you need to do is turn this immense bowl of dough into 48 almost equally immense cookies. Make balls of dough about twice the size of golf balls and place 12 balls on each cookie sheet, spacing them evenly. Having all the sheets in front of you will help you make sure the cookies are all the same size.

Bake one cookie sheet at a time on the middle rack in the oven. Bake the cookies for 11 minutes, reversing the sheet halfway through the baking. The cookies will not appear done at that point, but you just have to take them out anyway. (The surfaces of the cookies will be covered with small cracks, but inside the cracks, the cookies will still look wet.) If the bottoms are brown, you've baked the cookies too long.

Let the cookies cool right on the parchment-covered cookie sheet rather than transferring to racks; if you transfer them while they're still hot, they may drip down through the racks and make a horrible mess. (If you've cheated and not used the parchment paper, you should transfer the cookies after they've cooled for a few minutes. But really, you should use the paper.)

Once the cookies are cool, put them into plastic bags and store them in the freezer. Kept at room temperature, they dry out too fast. (In my family, we actually eat them straight from the freezer. They don't seem as deadly that way.)

Makes 48 large cookies.

To turn these into

The Only Oatmeal-Raisin Cookies

Substitute 8 ounces of *milk* chocolate for the semisweet chocolate you grind up with the oatmeal.

Cream the butter with granulated sugar and dark brown sugar instead of light brown. Instead of using the 24 ounces of chocolate chips, work in with your hands:

- **2 more cups old-fashioned rolled oats (not ground)**
- **1 15-ounce box raisins**
- **2 cups chopped walnuts**

(Using milk chocolate is important here. The raisins just don't go well with dark chocolate.)

Shape and bake as above.

Grandma Weld's Cookies

I DON'T KNOW who Grandma Weld is, or was. My mother got this recipe from someone at church or somewhere, and it's become one of the most asked-for recipes I've ever made. I feel a little guilty stealing the credit for it, and will be happy to make a public apology to Grandma Weld if she will only step forward.

If you can't find miniature chocolate chips—and I'm having more and more trouble with that—don't substitute regular chocolate chips. Bigger chips would make the cookies too sweet. Instead, stir in a cup of very finely chopped (not grated) unsweetened chocolate.

1	cup (2 sticks) unsalted butter, softened
⅓	cup sugar
2	cups all-purpose flour
2	teaspoons almond extract (this is the correct amount)
⅛	teaspoon salt
1	cup miniature chocolate chips

Cream the butter and sugar until light. Beat in the flour, almond extract and salt. Stir in the chocolate chips by hand.

Wrap the dough in plastic wrap or wax paper and chill it for at least 1 hour.

Preheat the oven to 300 degrees F. Shape the dough into 1 ½-inch-long "fingers" and place on ungreased cookie sheets. Bake for 15 to 20 minutes, watching carefully and breaking a couple of cookies open to check for doneness. The cookies should be cooked through, but they should not brown at all. Cool on racks and store in an airtight container.

Makes 5 dozen cookies.

Chocolate Ice Cream

FOR SOME REASON, chocolate never seems to taste as good in ice cream as it does in other desserts. One problem with many purchased chocolate ice creams is that they're made with cocoa, not chocolate. One problem with many *homemade* ice creams is that they're made with semisweet chocolate, not bitter chocolate. As far as I'm concerned, bitter chocolate lends a much better depth of flavor to ice cream. It's not as muddy, somehow. The following chocolate ice cream has all the depth of flavor even I could wish for.

6	ounces unsweetened chocolate, chopped fine
2	cups milk
¾	cup sugar
4	large egg yolks
	Pinch salt
2	cups heavy cream
1	teaspoon vanilla extract

Over low heat, whisk the unsweetened chocolate and 1 cup of the milk until the chocolate has melted and the mixture is smooth. Let the mixture cool.

In a small bowl, beat together the remaining 1 cup milk, sugar, egg yolks and salt until smooth and light. At the same time, scald the heavy cream. Whisk a dollop of hot cream into the egg mixture. Then pour the egg mixture into the cream and whisk well (while at the same time trying not to make the custard frothy). When the mixture is smooth, jettison the whisk in favor of a wooden spoon. Stirring constantly over very low heat, cook the mixture for 8 to 10 minutes, until it coats the spoon thickly. A candy thermometer will read 170 to 180 degrees F when the custard has been cooked enough. Add the cooled chocolate mixture and the vanilla.

Cool the custard to room temperature, about 20 minutes. I do this by carefully placing the saucepan into a larger pan of ice water and stirring until the mixture is cool enough. Because of all this chocolate, the custard will become too stiff to churn if it is actually chilled, so don't let it cool too much.

Freeze the custard according to your ice-cream maker's directions. Then transfer the custard—now ice cream, of course—to a sealed container. Leave it in your (regular) freezer overnight to mellow the flavor and firm the texture.

Makes 1 quart.

Helen Kenyon's Chocolate Sauce

IN THIS CASE, "the best" actually means "my husband's favorite." It *is* really good, though. At the place we go in Martha's Vineyard, they used to serve homemade vanilla ice cream every Sunday. Then they started using store ice cream—and it wasn't even Häagen-Dazs! Gyp! However, this sauce, which they kept on serving, almost kept us from noticing the change.

4	ounces unsweetened chocolate, chopped
1	tablespoon butter, melted
1½	cups sugar, preferably superfine
1	cup heavy cream
	Pinch salt
¼	cup dry sherry ("good" sherry, the original recipe cautions)
1	teaspoon vanilla extract

In a double boiler, melt the chocolate with the butter. Transfer to a heavy saucepan and combine the chocolate-butter mixture with the sugar, cream and salt. Over medium-low heat, stirring constantly, bring the mixture to a boil. Then allow it to boil slowly, without stirring, for 7 minutes. Remove the sauce from the heat and stir in the sherry and vanilla. Serve warm.

Store in the refrigerator.

Makes 2¾ cups.

Cinnamon Rolls

WELL, if *this* isn't an embarrassment to include here! But these are shockingly good. They're the only cinnamon rolls my family will eat. (I know that says something awful about us.) And at least they don't have any raisins in them. To my mind, there's nothing more cloying than cinnamon rolls with raisins. (Not that these cinnamon rolls aren't somewhat cloying, in their own way. I guess it's just a way that I love.)

2	tubes Pillsbury Refrigerated Dinner Rolls
¾	cup light brown sugar, packed
6	tablespoons (¾ stick) unsalted butter, softened
2	teaspoons cinnamon
¼	teaspoon freshly grated nutmeg

De-tube the dough, or whatever it's called. Unroll it into sheets and gently separate each sheet into 4 rectangles. Now you have a total of 8 rectangles.

Cream the sugar, butter, cinnamon and nutmeg until smooth.

Spread each rectangle with the sugar-butter mixture and roll up like a jelly roll, starting with the short end. Chill for at least ½ hour. (I always do this the night before.)

Preheat the oven to 375 degrees F.

Cut each roll of dough into 6 equal slices. Place these slices—which now, miraculously, have become rolls themselves!—close together in a 9-x-13-inch baking pan. They won't quite fill it, so make the pan a fake edge out of aluminum foil to tuck up next to the last row of rolls and keep them from getting all loose and sloppy.

Bake for 20 to 25 minutes; if you've chilled the rolls overnight, they may take ½ hour. They should all be well browned; it's probably only in my family that we like them half-raw.

Makes 48 little rolls, enough for my family of 4. (I'm not kidding.)

A Few Thoughts About Clam Chowder

I'M REALLY SORRY, GANG, but after long thought I've finally come down on the Manhattan side. (And I once wrote an article on clam chowder, so I actually did think about this for a long time.) I know, I know—preferring Manhattan chowder proves I'm not a purist. Okay, I guess I'm not. To me, even the best New England clam chowder has a tendency to taste like sea-flavored milk. I'm only even including a recipe for it because I have a lot of relatives in New England who would kill me if I didn't.

If you've ever prepared a Manhattan clam chowder the way most cookbooks suggest, though, I don't blame you for hating it. The commonest recipes recommend adding chopped stewed tomatoes to New England clam chowder. Stewed tomatoes in *milk*? No, thank you. The **Joy of Cooking** version actually has ketchup. *Let's see*, this kind of thinking goes, *we'll take the B-Minor Mass and add an accordion solo...*

But once you've added a few tomatoes, why not add some other vegetables too? And with all those vegetables, you're going to want a broth-based stock, not a milk-based one, and as long as you've strayed so far from pure old New England, you might as well throw in a little Pernod. The final result is just about the opposite of ketchup.

Recipes for both New England and Manhattan chowders are generally clam-poor. Nothing makes me angrier than spooning through vats of broth and turning up just potatoes, so in both my recipes I've doubled the standard quantity of clams.

"*Just* in the refridge," my fish dealer told me when I asked him how best to store my clams. You mean you're not supposed to let them sit in saltwater and cornmeal overnight to fatten them and purge them of sand and other impurities? "*Just* in the refridge," he repeated wearily.

Nevertheless, I tested the theory, giving half my clams a cornmeal bath and leaving the other half just in the refrigerator. The cornmealed clams didn't disgorge noticeable quantities of sand, but they did seem less scary inside when I chopped them. Besides, I like to imagine that I'm doing something nice for my clams before I kill them.

If you, too, want to give your condemned clams a last meal, scrub them thoroughly with a stiff brush. Then put them in a big kettle and cover them with a gallon of water mixed with ⅓ cup salt. Stir in a handful of cornmeal and put the clams into the refrigerator for 3 hours. Drain them, scrub them again, and proceed.

Manhattan Clam Chowder

4	dozen littleneck clams, scrubbed and "bathed" (see above)
2	cups water
½	pound bacon, diced
1	large onion, chopped
1	large carrot, halved and sliced
1	large leek, sliced
1	bay leaf
½	teaspoon dried thyme
1	15-ounce can plum tomatoes, chopped but undrained
2	cups boiling potatoes, scrubbed but unpeeled, cut into ½-inch cubes
1	cup heavy cream
	Salt and fresh-ground black pepper
2	tablespoons Pernod or ouzo
¼	cup finely chopped fresh parsley

Place the clams into a big kettle with the water. Bring to a boil and steam, covered, for 5 minutes. Discard any unopened clams. Remove the clams from their shells.

Reserving the broth, chop the clams coarsely and set aside. Through a fine strainer lined with a clean dish towel, strain the broth into a bowl.

In the soup pot you're using, fry the bacon until the fat is rendered and the bacon is barely brown. Drain off most of the fat, leaving enough to sauté the vegetables. Add the onions, carrots and leeks. Cook, stirring frequently, until tender but not browned. Add the bay leaf and thyme. Cook 5 minutes more.

Add 3 cups of the clam broth, the tomatoes and the potatoes. Simmer, covered, for 15 minutes.

"Nothing makes me angrier than spooning through vats of broth and turning up just potatoes."

Add the clams and simmer for 10 minutes or less. Do not allow the liquid to boil.

Add the heavy cream and stir over a very low flame until the soup is heated through. Season to taste with salt and pepper and add the Pernod or ouzo. Remove the bay leaf.

This soup will taste better if it's allowed to rest in the refrigerator overnight. Reheat it slowly and sprinkle with parsley just before serving.

Serves 4.

And if you insist . . .

New England Clam Chowder

Thickening the broth with flour and adding cream are not considered New England-y. On the other hand, how authentic do you want to be? Even real New Englanders no longer endure two-hour sermons in freezing meeting houses. Like the rest of us, they will secretly prefer a chowder whose edges have been slightly gilded.

4   dozen littleneck clams, scrubbed and "bathed" (see page 85)
2   cups water
6   ounces salt pork, rind removed, blanched and chopped
3   tablespoons unsalted butter
2   large onions, diced
3   tablespoons all-purpose flour
4   cups boiling potatoes, scrubbed but unpeeled, cut into ½-inch cubes
2   cups heavy cream
1   cup milk
    Fresh-ground black pepper (optional)

Place the clams in a large kettle with the water. Bring water to a boil and steam, covered, for 5 minutes. Discard any unopened clams. Remove the clams from their shells.

Reserving the broth, coarsely chop the clams. Through a fine strainer lined with a clean dish towel, strain the broth into a bowl.

Fry the salt pork in the soup pot over medium heat until the fat is rendered and the pork begins to brown. Add up to 2 tablespoons of the butter, if needed, to keep the pork from sticking. Remove the salt pork and add the onions, sautéing gently until they are soft and translucent. Add the flour and stir over low heat for 5 minutes without browning.

Add 3 cups of the reserved clam broth and the cubed potatoes. Simmer, covered, for 15 minutes. Add clams and simmer very gently until tender, 10 minutes or less.

Add cream, milk and the remaining 1 tablespoon butter. Stir constantly over a low flame until heated through. Do not allow the soup to boil. Add the optional pepper.

Serve immediately, or better, chill overnight; reheat slowly the next day.

Serves 4.

Coffee Ice Cream

I**T'S NOT EASY TO IMPROVE** on superpremium coffee ice cream. As a matter of fact, I'm not sure I've succeeded, though I do think this is just as good in a different way. Given the excellence of some commercial brands, I decided that the only direction to go in was to intensify the coffeeness in my recipe. You can even coffee it up a little more if you want.

As for the actual coffee, use whatever is your favorite. I use ground espresso beans. Decaffeinated, because I am a wuss.

This recipe must be started a day ahead, and you'll need an ice-cream maker.

1	cup milk
1	cup good-quality fine-ground coffee
1	tablespoon instant coffee (or more, if you want)
1	tablespoon dark rum
1	teaspoon vanilla extract
6	large egg yolks
½	cup sugar
	Pinch salt
3	cups heavy cream

Bring the milk to a boil and stir in the coffee. Let the mixture cool completely. Line a sieve with a coffee filter and drip the mixture into a bowl. When it stops dripping on its own, press down hard on the coffee with a spoon to extract every drop of black gold you can. Whisk in the instant coffee, rum and vanilla.

In a medium bowl, whisk the egg yolks, sugar and salt together until light. Meanwhile, heat the cream to a simmer. Whisk a dollop of cream slowly into the yolk mixture. Then whisk the egg mixture into the remaining cream. (Do not let the mixture get foamy.) Over very low heat, stirring constantly, cook the custard for 8 to 10 minutes. If you have a candy thermometer, use it: the custard should reach 170 to 180 degrees F. As soon as it begins to thicken, remove it from the heat.

Stir in the coffee infusion you've made.

Taste the mixture and see if it's coffee-ish enough for you. (Remember that freezing will mute the flavor slightly.) If you want a stronger flavor, you can dissolve another tablespoon or two of coffee into another tablespoon of rum and stir it in.

Cool the custard, then chill it thoroughly as for Vanilla Ice Cream (page 191).

Freeze the custard in an ice-cream maker according to the manufacturer's directions. Then transfer the custard—now ice cream, of course—to a sealed container. Leave it in your (regular) freezer overnight to mellow the flavor and firm the texture.

Makes 1 quart.

Kuchen (Coffeecake)

THIS, my godmother Ruth Atwater's recipe, is what my family always has on Christmas mornings. My first Christmas away from home, I was shocked to realize that Aunt Ruth, who lived in Rochester, would not be able to deliver me my own kuchen in Manhattan. Since Christmas couldn't be allowed to proceed without kuchen, I would have to learn to make it myself.

I have other tragic memories of that first New York Christmas, which was also my first married Christmas. My new husband actually *played a record* on Christmas night. A record! When (according to my family's traditions) you're supposed to pretend electricity doesn't *exist* at Christmastime! And he wanted *lights* on the tree instead of candles! And he thought that I should relax and enjoy the holiday instead of working myself to death cleaning house and making 50 kinds of Christmas cookies we wouldn't eat! Well, the customs of other cultures often seem bizarre at first.

The first time I tried making this kuchen, I got confused by the directions. The recipe makes two kuchen rings, which I somehow thought were supposed to be baked together in the same pan. Naturally they didn't bake at all. When I sliced into the result, a great lava-like rush of hot dough poured out. The following year, I had the idea that you were supposed to pinch the dough into a tube shape, with all the filling inside: Christmas cannoli. I think I've got it down now, but the original recipe has almost disappeared under all my marginalia and underlinings.

Dough

¾	cup milk, scalded
⅓	cup (5 ⅓ tablespoons) unsalted butter
¼	cup sugar plus 1 tablespoon
½	teaspoon salt
3	large eggs, well beaten
½	teaspoon vanilla extract
2	packages active dry yeast
½	cup lukewarm water
	Pinch ginger
4	cups sifted all-purpose flour

Filling

1	cup raisins (simmered for 10 minutes in 1 cup water, then drained and dried)
1	cup slivered almonds
½	cup light brown sugar, packed
1	large egg, well beaten
1	tablespoon heavy cream

Glaze

¾	cup confectioners' sugar
1	tablespoon hot cream
¼	teaspoon vanilla extract

Dough: In a large bowl (preferably the bowl of an electric mixer with a dough hook), pour the scalded milk over the butter, and add ¼ cup of the sugar and the salt. When the butter has melted, slowly add the well-beaten eggs and the vanilla.

Dissolve the yeast in the lukewarm water with the remaining 1 tablespoon of sugar and the ginger. Let the yeast proof for 10 minutes; then add the yeast mixture to the milk mixture. Add the flour gradually, while beating, until the dough is smooth.

Knead (again, preferably with a dough hook) until the dough is no longer sticky—at least 5 or 10 minutes. Transfer the dough to a clean, buttered bowl. Cover the bowl with a clean, damp cloth and set it in a warm place until the dough has doubled in bulk—about 2 hours. Punch the dough down and let rise, covered, until doubled once more. Then punch the dough down, cover it, and chill it overnight. This will, theoretically, make it easier to work with.

In the morning, heavily butter two 9-inch round cake pans. Punch down the chilled dough if it needs it, and divide the dough in half. On a well-floured surface, roll out half the dough into a rough rectangle ½ inch thick. Place this rectangle in the refrigerator and repeat the process with the second piece of dough, which you can leave on the work surface while you prepare the filling.

Filling: (This must be mixed as close as possible to the time it will be used; it liquefies fast.) Mix together the raisins, almonds, brown sugar, egg and cream.

Spread half the filling on the rolled-out dough, leaving a ½-inch margin along the long sides and a ¼-inch margin at the ends. Then roll up the dough like a jelly roll, starting with the long side of the rectangle. Roll as tightly as possible, sweating with fear and tension. Why did you decide to make this for Christmas breakfast? Didn't you have enough to do already?

"Why did you decide to make this for Christmas breakfast? Didn't you have enough to do already?"

Carefully place the rolled-up dough, seam-side up, in one of the greased cake pans and pinch the "open" ends hard to seal them together, making a ring. With scissors or a sharp knife, cut inch-deep slashes into the dough at intervals around the ring. This should form florets, my godmother says.

Repeat the process with the second piece of dough, *in a second pan*. Allow both kuchen to come to room temperature. Preheat the oven to 400 degrees F. Bake the kuchen for 20 to 25 minutes, or until they are well browned on top. Use the point of a small, sharp knife to make sure the dough is cooked all the way through. As the kuchen bake, prepare the glaze by whisking the ingredients together until they're smooth.

Take the finished kuchen out of the oven and spread the glaze over them right away while they're still hot. Unless you are planning to eat the kuchen that day (and you'd have to get up pretty early in the morning for them to be done by breakfast), let them cool, then wrap them in plastic wrap and freeze them. I always take one out to thaw the night before the morning I plan to serve it. (I usually give the prettier of the two away.) Then I reheat the kuchen, covered in foil, for about 10 minutes at 300 degrees.

Makes two 9-inch kuchen, each one serving 6.

These freeze very well.

Corn Bread

WHEN IT COMES to corn bread, I'm an unrepentant Northerner. I like it with yellow cornmeal, and I like it with sugar. This recipe produces a nice tall loaf of bread, if "loaf" is what you say when you bake it in a skillet. It also keeps better than most corn breads. It also tastes better, unless you're a Southerner.

½   cup (1 stick) unsalted butter, softened, plus extra for brushing the top
½   cup sugar
3   large eggs
1½ cups all-purpose flour
1½ cups stone-ground yellow cornmeal
2   tablespoons baking powder
¾   teaspoon salt
1½ cups milk

Preheat the oven to 425 degrees F. Butter a 9-inch cast-iron skillet generously.

In a large bowl, cream the butter and sugar for 10 minutes. (It helps if you have a stand-up mixer so you can roam the kitchen during this period.) Beat in the eggs, one at a time.

In a small bowl, stir together the flour, cornmeal, baking powder and salt. Add these dry ingredients to the butter mixture alternately with the milk, beginning and ending with the dry ingredients.

Place the skillet in the preheated oven until it is hot. Then take the skillet out and turn the batter into it. Bake for 30 to 35 minutes, or until the bread is browned on top and a cake tester comes out clean.

The minute the corn bread is out of the oven, brush the top with a teaspoon or so of melted butter. Or you can just drop a pat of butter on top and push it around until the surface of the corn bread is coated.

Serves 6 to 8.

Jalapeño Corn Bread

I ALWAYS serve this when we're having barbecued spareribs. It's nicely spicy and it has the most gorgeous texture of any corn bread.

2 **large eggs**
1 **cup sour cream**
⅓ **cup corn oil**
1 **cup cream-style canned corn**
¾ **cup fresh or frozen (defrosted) corn kernels**
1 **cup stone-ground yellow cornmeal**
1 **tablespoon baking powder**
1 **teaspoon salt**
¼ **cup grated extra-sharp Cheddar**
2 **tablespoons canned drained jalapeño pepper, minced (If you suddenly get the impulse to rub your eyes after handling jalapeños—or to rub your eyes with the jalapeños themselves—don't do it. Wear gloves when you work with any hot pepper.)**

Preheat the oven to 375 degrees F. Butter a 9-x-13-inch pan.

Beat the eggs in a large bowl. Then beat in the sour cream, oil, creamed corn and corn kernels. In a small bowl, combine the cornmeal, baking powder and salt; beat them into the sour-cream mixture.

Stir in the cheese and jalapeños. Pour the batter into the pan and bake for ½ hour, or until golden. Serve immediately.

Serves 6 to 8.

Corn on the Cob

MY MOTHER was once at a house where the hostess left the living room to check on the broccoli. In a minute she returned. "Just one more hour," she announced.

I plowed through many of my older cookbooks hoping to find a corn-on-the-cob recipe that called for endless boiling, so I could make fun of it. Unfortunately, I didn't find one. Most of the recipes were in the 5-to-10-minute category. But that's still way too long for fresh corn. A minute or two is fine.

Get the freshest corn you can.

While you're husking the corn, bring a large pot of water to the boil.

If the corn is the silvery, delicate, pearl-like kind, boil it for 1 minute. If it's the horsey, yellow, stick-between-your teeth kind, boil it for 2 minutes. All you really want to do is to heat it through.

Drain and serve, wrapped in a towel—the corn, I mean.

Crab Cakes

GENERALLY I'M WARY of any recipe that mushes seafood and crumbs together. The results are too often bland, gloppy excuses for stretching out the fish and eating something fried. But I'd never ask you to do something like that, would I?

You do have to use fresh crabmeat, so don't think you can get away with those little cans of Geisha. That's something only our mothers would do. (And then they'd serve the crab cakes with some nice frozen corn. You, of course, will serve them with endive and watercress salad.)

Crab Cakes

1	cup fine fresh breadcrumbs
2	large eggs, lightly beaten
¼	cup mayonnaise
¼	cup minced onion
1	large clove garlic, minced
4	tablespoons minced fresh parsley
½	teaspoon salt
¼	teaspoon dry mustard
¼	teaspoon cayenne
1	pound FRESH! crabmeat, picked over
	All-purpose flour for dredging the cakes
2	tablespoons corn oil

Orange Sauce

2	shallots, minced
1	cup orange juice (boiled until reduced to ¼ cup)
¼	cup dry white wine
¼	cup (½ stick) unsalted butter, cut into bits
¼	cup heavy cream

Crab cakes: Preheat the oven to 200 degrees F. Combine the crumbs, eggs, mayonnaise, onion, garlic and seasonings. Stir in the crabmeat gently. Shape mixture into 4 patties; dredge them in flour. (They will be tender, so handle them carefully.) Heat the oil until very hot and cook the patties for 5 minutes on each side, or until brown and sizzling. Remove and keep warm in the oven while you make the orange sauce.

Orange sauce: In a stainless-steel or enameled saucepan, boil the shallots, reduced juice and wine together until the liquid is reduced to ¼ cup. Using a wire whisk, whisk in the butter bit by bit until it is all absorbed. The sauce will be almost as thick as a mayonnaise. Remove the pan from the heat and whisk in the cream.

Technically, this crab cake recipe serves 4. However, you might as well go ahead and double it. You should also double the Orange Sauce that accompanies it, since people tend to eat it with their spoons if you turn your back for even a second.

Although the butter and cream should be whisked in at the last minute, the first part of the sauce—the shallots, wine and reduced juice—may be prepared ahead of time and reheated for the last steps. To make this sauce the *absolute*, undoubted best, it should of course be prepared with freshly squeezed orange juice. However, I never bother with that if I've got concentrate in the fridge, because the juice is reduced so much that such nuances vanish by the time the sauce is done. It *is* okay to cheat when no one catches you, isn't it?

Soft-Shelled Crabs

Y OU SHOULD REALLY buy soft-shelled crabs alive and kill them yourself, but it's hard to do: cutting off a living creature's face just isn't pleasant. Once I bought some soft-shells at a fish store and the woman in charge asked me if I wanted them killed or not. I didn't want to say, "*You* have to kill them," so instead I said, "Why don't you show me how to do it and then I can do it myself from now on?" I didn't especially like seeing how to do it, though. The next time I went into the store to buy soft-shells I didn't say anything about killing them myself. Unfortunately, the woman remembered me and gave me live crabs without asking me which kind I wanted. I didn't have the guts to ask her to kill them *again*, so I had to do it myself. The fish store closed soon after that, luckily.

Now that I've whetted your appetite, let me say that the only way to serve soft-shelled crabs is with lemon juice and almonds. There is no other.

¼	cup all-purpose flour
	Salt and fresh-ground black pepper
	A "shake" of cayenne
6	soft-shelled crabs, cleaned and dried
½	cup (1 stick) unsalted butter
1	tablespoon corn oil
½	cup sliced almonds
	Juice from 1 large lemon
1	tablespoon minced fresh parsley

Season the flour with the salt, pepper and cayenne. Put the flour into a shallow pan and lightly coat the crabs with it, brushing off any excess.

Heat the butter and oil in a large, heavy skillet. Cook the crabs in batches over medium-high heat for 3 to 4 minutes on each side, or until they are golden brown. Put the crabs onto a hot platter.

Stir the almonds into the butter and oil remaining in the skillet and cook them until they, too, are golden brown. Pour the lemon juice and parsley into the skillet and stir quickly, scraping the skillet to get up as many brown bits as you can. As soon as everything is combined, pour the sauce over the crabs and serve immediately.

Serves 2 or 3 people, depending on the size of the crabs (and the people).

Cranberry Jelly

YOU MAKE A SMALL flavor sacrifice when you serve cranberry jelly instead of cranberry sauce. In cooking the berries long enough to make them moldable, you turn them less juicy and hence slightly less perky-tasting. But you're probably the only one who will notice it. Cranberry jelly, after all, is rarely savored on its own in tiny spoonfuls. It's more likely to be shoveled into a sludge of turkey, stuffing and mashed potatoes. And even if someone at your table *is* eating the jelly plain (like my children, for instance, who don't like any of the other elements of Thanksgiving dinner), they probably won't say, "Hey! This cranberry jelly tastes slightly less perky than cranberry sauce!"

Besides, your own cranberry jelly tastes better and is a lot prettier than the canned kind. When did it become okay to serve canned cranberry jelly still in its canned shape? Granted, it's fun to make that schwupping sound when you slide the jelly out of the can, but aren't you supposed to chop the jelly up a little before you put it on the table? Or has that can-shaped red torpedo now become a Thanksgiving tradition all its own?

SPECIAL BONUS CRANBERRY TIP: If you make cranberry-orange relish instead of cranberry jelly, try adding a little almond extract to your usual recipe. It makes a big difference.

1   pound fresh cranberries
2   cups water
2   cups sugar
     Pinch salt

Wash and pick over the cranberries, discarding the stems and what my kids call "softies." Bring the water to a boil and add the cranberries, sugar and salt. Boil for a long, long time—at least ½ hour—skimming the froth off the top when you think of it. Stir frequently to avoid scorching. When the cranberries are done enough, they will be noticeably thick and syrupy; dripped off the side of the spoon, two drops will combine into one; and dripped into ice water, a blob of jelly will hold its shape (about 200 to 210 degrees F on a candy thermometer).

Pour the jelly into a wet mold, preferably a metal one. Chill it until serving time. When it's time to unmold the jelly, fill the sink with hot water and send everyone out of the kitchen so they won't see you tensing up. Hold the mold in the water for a few seconds, until you start to see moisture around the edges of the jelly. Then upend it onto a plate. If it doesn't work the first time, just heat the mold again. If it spills out in a big liquidy burst and gets all over everything, you didn't cook it long enough.

If it *never* comes out of the mold, you can scoop out spoonfuls and try to arrange them nicely in a bowl. People will see that you tried hard.

Makes 4 cups.

Dog Biscuits

I'M INCLUDING THESE because they make great stocking-stuffers for dog-owners. They're also a nice addition to a bake sale—especially in my neighborhood, where people think you're a Communist if you don't own some kind of retriever.

Gerbils like them too.

3½	cups all-purpose flour
2	cups whole-wheat flour
1	cup rye flour
2	cups cracked wheat or Wheatena cereal, uncooked, straight from the box
2	teaspoons salt
1	package active dry yeast
2	cups beef stock or consommé
½	cup milk
2	large eggs

Preheat the oven to 325 degrees F.

In a large bowl, mix together the flours, the cracked wheat or Wheatena, the salt and the yeast; stir in the beef stock or consommé, the milk and the eggs. (The dough will be very stiff and heavy.) Knead with your hands until well mixed, then roll out to a thickness of ¼ to 1 inch on a lightly floured board. With scissors or a sharp knife, cut into 1-inch squares and place the squares on a lightly greased cookie sheet. (They don't spread, so you can put them close together. Usually I have to make three cookie sheets' worth and freeze on the sheets to bake the next day.)

Bake for 45 minutes. Then turn off the oven and leave the biscuits in the oven overnight or for 8 hours. Store the biscuits airtight.

Makes 20 dozen.

Bacony Deviled Eggs

WHAT COULD BE A MORE LOGICAL PLACE to put bacon than in a deviled egg? But every time you do it, people marvel.

12	large eggs, hard-boiled, peeled and carefully sliced in half
½	cup mayonnaise
¼	cup sour cream
1	tablespoon Dijon mustard
1	tablespoon prepared white horseradish, or to taste
8	ounces bacon, cooked crisp, drained and crumbled fine
4	scallions, chopped fine

Plop the egg yolks into a small bowl and mash them with the back of a spoon until smooth. Then stir in the mayonnaise, sour cream, mustard and horseradish. When the yolk mixture is smooth, make it bumpy again by stirring in the bacon and the scallions. Taste for seasoning.

Using two spoons, stuff the egg whites with the yolk mixture. Don't think you can use a pastry bag fitted with a star tip for *this* recipe. I tried it once, and the scallions and bacon kept getting stuck in the points of the star.

It's just as well you can't make fancy piped eggs, though, because now you can cover them with plastic wrap more easily. Keep them covered and chilled until you're ready to serve them.

Putting deviled eggs—the slipperiest food known to man— on a bed of parsley is supposed to keep them from sliding around the platter. But the only way to make that work is to use a whole lot of parsley; you'd need a couple of bags, not just a sprig or two. And even then your eggs wouldn't necessarily be kept from tipping over if you had to take them in the car. If I have to drive deviled eggs somewhere, I line a tray with a sheet of plastic wrap. Then I put the eggs in little nests of scrunched-up plastic wrap, making sure that each nest is touching its neighbor. I then cover the platter with more plastic wrap, and those guys stay where they're supposed to. When I get to, say, my friends Nora and Dave's annual Derby Party, I take away all the plastic wrap except for the sheet lining the bottom of the tray. Then I put the eggs on, and last of ˉ¹l enough parsley to hide the plastic wrap.

This plastic-wrap method also works very well for transporting other foods. A plate of cupcakes won't slide off their moorings, either, if you tuck plastic wrap around each one. And if you have to take fragile cookies or a frosted cake somewhere in a box—a task I don't envy you—you can place a wreath of crumpled plastic wrap all around the cake (or cookies) and in the box corners.

But back to the eggs. Of course I've been wasting my breath if you already own one of those indented egg platters. If you do, go ahead and serve the eggs in it, for God's sake!

You will have 24 of them to serve.

English French Toast

THE BEST FRENCH TOAST, I think, is the one that sponges up the most custard and still holds its shape. Once I tried French-toasting slices of pound cake, but they dissolved into a soggy mass of crumbs when it came time to lift them out of the bowl. Other breads didn't seem to want to absorb anything; I had to slash great gashes in bagels before they would submit even to sniff the custard.

English muffins are nicely porous, and they're also unlikely to fall apart—so they can soak for much longer than the average French toast dip-ee. Of course they need to be soaking in something worth soaking in. Since I don't like maple syrup very much, I make my French toast slightly sweet. (Adding sugar also makes the French toast brown better.) A sprinkling of confectioners' sugar is all you need on French toast prepared this way, but if you *have* to have maple syrup, just decrease the sugar in the custard.

Many cookbooks recommend using day-old bread to make French toast. This seems disingenuous to me. I think we can safely assume that unless you made your English muffins an hour ago, they are at least one day old.

4	large eggs
1	cup milk
½	cup heavy cream
¼	cup sugar (preferably superfine)
1	teaspoon cinnamon
⅛	teaspoon freshly grated nutmeg
	Pinch salt
½	teaspoon grated orange rind
¼	teaspoon vanilla extract
4	English muffins, split
½	cup (1 stick) unsalted butter (you may not need it all)

Beat the eggs well, and add the milk and cream. Beat well again, and add the sugar. Beat until the sugar is all dissolved. Then add the cinnamon, nutmeg, salt, orange rind and vanilla.

Pour the custard into a 9-x-13-inch pan.

Split the muffins in half using two forks or your fingers. (The rough surface of an English muffin is part of the reason it tastes good.) Prick each muffin half with a fork in a few places. Place them rough-side down in the custard for 10 minutes. With a spatula, turn them over carefully and let them soak for another 10 minutes.

Preheat the oven to 200 degrees F.

Over a medium-low flame, heat 4 tablespoons of the butter in a large, heavy skillet. When the butter is bubbling, carefully transfer 4 of the muffin halves to the skillet. Cook them gently until they are golden brown on the bottom; then turn them and fry the other side until it, too, is golden brown. Keep the first 4 muffin-halves warm in the oven while you cook the other 4.

Serve the French toast immediately.

Serves 4.

Perfect Fudge (if you're lucky)

A PERFECT PIECE OF FUDGE is velvety and sugary at the same time. It doesn't quite melt in your mouth, and you don't want it to. You want it to resist your bite ever so slightly: to remain faintly chewy, like the ghost of a caramel, before it finally gives way to luxurious creaminess. That's why I hate nuts in my fudge: they get in the way of that elusive textural perfection.

My problem has always been that 50 percent of the fudge I make turns out creamy and luxurious, and 50 percent turns out like chips of flint.

You don't have much chance of screwing up those fudges based on Marshmallow Fluff. (They always have names like "First Lady's Fudge" or "Million-Dollar-Fudge.") On the other hand, they're usually too sweet—one recipe I saw called for five pounds of sugar—and often they're gummy as well.

You *do* have a chance of screwing up this recipe, alas. Because it has more chocolate and more butterfat than most fudges, it's temperamental. But if you treat it very respectfully and don't overbeat it and don't make it on a damp day and don't let the chocolate scorch and don't scrape the pan when you're pouring the fudge and don't do all the other things that make fudge cranky, you'll find this fudge sublime. (To use a food-writerly word.)

2	cups superfine sugar
1	cup heavy cream
5	tablespoons unsalted butter
3	ounces bitter (unsweetened) chocolate, chopped
1	tablespoon light corn syrup
⅛	teaspoon salt
1	teaspoon vanilla extract

Butter an 8-inch-square pan. In a heavy 3-quart saucepan whose sides you have buttered, combine the superfine sugar, heavy cream, butter, chocolate, corn syrup and the salt. Stirring constantly, bring to a boil over low heat.

When the mixture reaches a boil, cover tightly and continue to cook for 3 minutes. (This will help to "steam down" any sugar crystals that might form on the sides of the pan.) Uncover; place a candy thermometer in the mixture; and slowly boil, stirring occasionally, until the mixture reaches 236 degrees F.

Immediately place the pan into a sink filled with 1 inch of cold (not ice) water. Pour the vanilla over the top of the mixture, but do not stir it in.

Cool the pan, without touching it, until the mixture reaches 110 degrees. Remove from the sink; dry off the bottom. Beat, either with a wooden spoon or with an electric hand mixer, until the mixture *begins* to lose its gloss and to offer *slight* resistance to the spoon or mixer. It's overbeating that produces those chips of flint.

Immediately pour the fudge mixture into the buttered pan. Don't scrape the fudge pot—just get as much fudge into the pan by pouring as you can. Cool the fudge at room temperature and cut it into squares.

Makes one 8-inch-square pan, about 1 ½ pounds.

Perfect Vanilla Fudge

The technique is exactly the same as above, but the ingredients are as follows:

2	cups superfine sugar
1	cup heavy cream
½	cup (1 stick) unsalted butter
1	tablespoon light corn syrup
⅛	teaspoon salt
1	teaspoon vanilla extract

Makes one 8-inch-square pan, about 1 ½ pounds.

"My problem has always been that 50 percent of the fudge I make turns out creamy and luxurious, and 50 percent turns out like chips of flint."

Hot Fudge Sauce

HOT FUDGE SAUCE is another thing people like to brag about. *Everyone's* hot fudge sauce is supposed to be the absolute richest, or the thickest or the most deeply, darkly divine. Mine is the most embarrassing. Once I gave a friend a jar of hot fudge sauce as a present. I labeled it simply "Hot Fudge," thinking the fact that it was in a *jar* would make it clear it was a sauce. Wouldn't that be clear to you? But the next day there was a message from my friend on my answering machine. "My mouth is full of delicious hot fudge," he said. I have this awful feeling that he thought it was a kind of spoon-fudge he was supposed to eat from the jar. I never asked him about it, though. How could I? *You know that jar of hot fudge I gave you? You did use it on ice cream and not just eat it plain, right?*

Speaking of eating things plain brings me to the other time this sauce humiliated me. In college I once had a summer job as a live-in cook and housekeeper for an elderly couple. At that time in my life I was always on big, public diets, which I always ended up breaking in private. One such diet-break involved my eating half a jar of the fudge sauce this couple loved to have me make. I thought they had forgotten it was in the refrigerator, but unfortunately they hadn't. A couple of days later they asked where it was, and I pretended I didn't know. Then, of course, I had to make a new jar, eat it down to the same level and stash it in the dish cupboard "by accident." "Oh, look! I must have put this away in here without thinking!" I exclaimed the following week when I was taking down some cups.

Unfortunately, the man of the house came downstairs unexpectedly a few days after that and walked in on me. I was sitting in the kitchen eating fudge sauce out of the jar.

The recipe that caused me all this agitation is deeply, darkly divine too, but it's not the absolute richest. You have to save a *little* richness for the ice cream.

3   ounces unsweetened chocolate, chopped
1   cup sugar
⅛   teaspoon salt
½   cup light corn syrup
½   cup heavy cream
3   tablespoons unsalted butter
1   tablespoon dry sherry
2   teaspoons vanilla extract

In a large, heavy saucepan, mix the chocolate, sugar, salt, corn syrup, heavy cream and butter. Bring to a boil, stirring constantly. Then turn the heat down to low and cook the sauce for 15 minutes, stirring frequently. The sauce should be quite thick.

Cool the sauce to room temperature. Stir in the sherry and vanilla, and start eating the sauce out of the jar.

Makes 1 pint.

Gingerbread

THIS GINGERBREAD has been one of my favorites forever. For some reason, I always baked it when the staff of my high-school literary magazine was coming over to discuss which submissions we should publish in the magazine.

Why did I think a homely dessert like gingerbread was a good thing to feed high-school aesthetes? I don't know, but it always got eaten.

½	cup (1 stick) unsalted butter, softened
1	cup sugar
2	large eggs, well beaten
1	cup milk
1	cup "light" molasses (I mean mild in flavor, not lite in calories; you don't want blackstrap here)
2 ½	cups all-purpose flour
½	teaspoon baking soda
⅛	teaspoon salt
1	tablespoon ginger
½	teaspoon cinnamon
¼	teaspoon cloves
¼	teaspoon freshly grated nutmeg

Preheat the oven to 350 degrees F. Butter a 9-x-13-inch baking pan and line the bottom with parchment paper cut to fit.

Cream together the butter and the sugar. Add the eggs and mix well. Add the milk and the molasses (which will be much easier to pour if you grease the measuring cup before pouring in the molasses). Now sift the dry ingredients into this messy-looking liquid and beat well. Pour the batter into the greased pan.

Bake for 30 to 35 minutes, or until the gingerbread begins to pull away slightly from the sides of the pan. Cool on a rack and serve warm or cold. This keeps well, freezes well and makes a nice breakfast.

Makes one 9-x-13-inch pan of gingerbread, which you may cut into whatever size you like.

Gingersnaps

I WAS ALL SET to run my great-grandmother's gingersnap recipe here. And I was going to tell you about how we used to make her cookies every Christmas, and then hang them on the tree, and *that* would have reminded me of the time my parents were taking care of an iguana for some friends, and he got out of his tank and ran up the Christmas tree . . .

And then my conscience won, and I realized that the Lemon-Ginger cookies in **The Silver Palate Good Times Cookbook** are *way* better than my great-grandmother's, iguana or no iguana. Lemon-Ginger Cookies are a timeless work of art, whereas Great-Grandma Minnie's cookies were just rolled out very thin.

- ½ **cup (1 stick) unsalted butter, at room temperature**
- ⅔ **cup sugar**
- 2 **tablespoons light brown sugar, packed**
- ¼ **cup pure maple syrup**
  Rind from 1 lemon, finely grated
  Juice from 1 lemon
- 1 **teaspoon orange extract**
- 1 **cup cake flour**
- 1 **teaspoon ginger**
- ½ **cup finely chopped crystallized ginger**

Preheat the oven to 325 degrees F. Line cookie sheets with foil and butter the foil.

Cream the butter and sugars in a large mixer bowl. Beat in the maple syrup, lemon rind and juice and orange extract.

Sift the flour and ginger together into another bowl. Add the finely chopped crystallized ginger and toss to coat. Stir this mixture into the butter mixture.

Drop teaspoons of the batter 3 inches apart on the prepared cookie sheets, leaving plenty of space for the cookies to spread. Bake the cookies one sheet at a time for 12 to 15 minutes, watching closely so they don't burn. They will be thin and lacy.

Let the cookies cool on the sheets "for about 4 minutes," **Good Times** instructs. Then lift them carefully off onto racks to finish cooling.

Makes 4 dozen cookies.

Grape Ice Cream

THIS IS A SHOCKING grape-bubble-gum color, but don't let that put you off. It doesn't taste like bubble gum at all, and once in a while it's nice to serve a food that's really, really purple.

1 cup sugar
½ cup water
1 ¼ cups unsweetened grape juice
1 cup (½ pint) heavy cream
1 large egg yolk
1 "shake" of salt

In a medium saucepan, over medium heat, stir together the sugar and water until they reach a boil. Boil slowly for 5 minutes.

Take the pan off the heat and stir in the grape juice. Cool the mixture.

In a separate saucepan, scald the cream. Whisk in the egg yolk and salt. Over low heat, and stirring constantly, cook the mixture until it is thick and forms a custard. (At the right temperature, a candy thermometer will register 170 to 180 degrees F.)

Pour the custard through a sieve into the grape juice mixture. Still well. Chill for several hours (or stir over ice until thoroughly cold, about 20 minutes).

Freeze the mixture in an ice-cream maker according to the manufacturer's directions.

Makes 1 scant quart.

Grape Pie

RARELY do I run into people who are hunting for the best grape pie recipe ever. But I like grape pie so much that I'm sneaking it in. Call it "Best Use of Concord Grape Skins," if you want.

Pastry

2 ½	cups all-purpose flour
1	teaspoon grated lemon rind
¼	teaspoon salt
1	cup (2 sticks) unsalted butter, softened
¼	cup Crisco
5	tablespoons ice water
1	teaspoon vanilla extract

Filling

4	cups Concord grapes
1 ⅓	cups sugar
3	tablespoons cornstarch
2	tablespoons unsalted butter, melted
1	tablespoon plus 1 teaspoon fresh lemon juice

Glaze

	Milk
1	tablespoon sugar

Pastry: Preheat the oven to 350 degrees F.

Stir together the flour, lemon rind and salt. Cut in the butter and Crisco using whatever pie-crust method works best for you. (I use a pastry blender.) When the mixture resembles coarse meal, sprinkle in the ice water and the vanilla. Gently gather the dough into a ball with a fork. Divide it into sort-of halves. (One half should be a little bigger than the other half.) Press each "half" into a disk about 1 inch thick. Wrap each disk in plastic wrap and chill for ½ hour. While they're getting cold, make the filling.

Filling and assembly: Stem the grapes and slip them out of their skins. (Save the skins. You need them.) Bring the little blobby grape insides to a simmer over low heat; simmer them for 5 minutes. Immediately sieve the grape pulp to remove the seeds. Let the pulp cool while you make the bottom crust.

Butter the bottom and sides of a 9-inch pie pan. On a floured rolling surface, roll out the smaller "half" of dough until it forms a circle about 12 inches in diameter. Line the pie pan with the dough, being careful not to stretch the dough. Stick the pan in the refrigerator for 15 minutes.

Butter the shiny side of a 14-inch square of aluminum foil. Place the foil, butter-side down, in the pastry-lined pie pan. Fill it with 2 cups of pie weights, raw rice or dried beans. Bake the shell on a cookie sheet for 20 minutes. Transfer to a rack. Remove the pie weights and foil and cool the crust.

As the crust cools slightly, roll out the other disk of dough into a circle about 13 inches in diameter. This time you can just let it sit; you'll need it in a minute.

Combine the grape pulp and grape skins. Stir together the sugar and cornstarch and add to the grapes. Then stir in the melted butter and lemon juice.

Spoon the filling into the pie shell. Top with the second crust and crimp the two crusts together. Cut several holes in the top crust to let the steam out.

Glaze: Quickly brush the pie with milk. Then sprinkle it with the 1 tablespoon of sugar.

Bake the pie on the bottom rack of the oven, on the cookie sheet, for 50 minutes. (The cookie sheet helps concentrate heat on the bottom of the pie pan, which in turn helps make the bottom crust flakier.) Then transfer the pie to the middle of the oven and bake it for another 10 minutes.

Cool slightly before cutting.

Makes one 9-inch pie.

"Call this 'Best Use of Concord Grape Skins,' if you want."

Great Gravy: Chicken and Beef

THE BEST WAY TO MAKE GRAVY is not to have been the person who cooked the rest of the meal. Gravy is of necessity a last-minute proposition—you can't make it until the meat is done—and when you've been spending a few hours putting together the kind of meal at which gravy is served, you're probably not willing to embark on a nerve-wracking last-minute venture. "Pan juices are fine," you find yourself thinking grumpily.

Still, every now and then you really can't get out of making gravy. Thanksgiving, Christmas, the local Gravy-a-thon at the town hall—you're stuck when these events roll around. So foist the job off on someone else, and read them these directions.

Don't foist the job off on my husband, though. Once he put baby formula in chicken gravy *on purpose*.

For any kind of gravy, you should brown the flour before you use it. (Browning the flour reduces the chance of the gravy's being pasty.) You can at least do *this* part ahead of time.

At some point during the baking of the large chunk of protein you're making all this fuss about, put a cup of flour into a pan and stick it in the oven for a few minutes, stirring occasionally. When it's light brown, it's done.

Next comes the question of the stock from which you'll be making the gravy. Normally, you have quarts of excellent stock on hand that you've made in your spare time, but let's assume that at the moment you don't. So you're starting from scratch. You don't yet have the carcass you could use to make stock, because it hasn't finished cooking, much less been eaten. You have to improvise. You have to doctor a saucepanful of water and make it interesting.

Chicken Gravy

6 tablespoons all-purpose flour, browned in the oven (see page 115)

Stock

	Chicken giblets and neck
2	large carrots, cut in chunks
2	large stalks celery, cut in chunks
2	large onions, cut in thick slabs
3	whole cloves garlic, peeled
1	teaspoon whole peppercorns
	Handful fresh parsley sprigs
2	teaspoons dried thyme
1	teaspoon dried sage
2	10-ounce cans chicken broth (Canned chicken broth, by the way, tastes much better than the broth you can make from bouillon cubes.)
2	cups water
½	cup dry vermouth or dry white wine

Put the giblets (not the liver) and neck into a large saucepan along with everything else. Bring to a boil. Then turn down the heat and let the stock simmer away for a couple of hours. Skim off the scum on the stock's surface every now and then, a nasty job if there ever was one. The stock should reduce by at least a quarter, or until you think it tastes full-flavored enough.

When the stock has reduced enough, pour it through a strainer lined with a clean dishtowel into another saucepan. (If I were you, I'd wait till no one was looking and just throw away the dishtowel when I was done with it.) Check the seasoning. If there's still lots of time before your chicken or turkey is done, let the stock cool. If it's time to take the damn thing out of the oven, keep the stock warm.

Transfer the bird to another plate, cover it with foil, and keep it warm. Call out nervously to your guests that everything is fine.

Now pour ¼ cup of chicken or turkey drippings into a medium saucepan. Scrape up as much as you can of the browned bits on the bottom of the pan in which the turkey has cooked, and add them to the drippings. Over low heat, stirring with a whisk, begin to heat the drippings and browned bits.

When the drippings begin to sizzle, stir in the 6 tablespoons of browned flour you made earlier. Whisk and whisk and whisk until the mixture begins to form a paste.

"The best way to make gravy is not to have been the person who cooked the rest of the meal."

Pour in 2 ½ cups of hot stock all at once. Immediately start whisking like crazy until the stock and the flour mixture are combined. Keeping the heat low, simmer the mixture for about 5 minutes. Then turn up the heat slightly and cook, whisking often, until the mixture has reached what can only be called a gravy-ish consistency. If it gets too thick, you can add a little more stock.

Check the seasonings and serve the gravy immediately. We don't have a nice gravy boat, so we pour it out of a china teapot. It actually works very well.

Makes 2 ½ cups gravy.

Beef Gravy

For beef gravy, the question of stock is a little more problematic. Rarely do people have beef bones around the house, unless they've bought a few for their dogs. If you have any leftover meats lying around in your refrigerator, you could add them. If not, don't worry about it too much.

- 6 tablespoons all-purpose flour, browned in the oven (see page 115)
  Any meat scraps you may have in your refrigerator (ones that aren't too disreputable)
- 2 large carrots, cut in chunks
- 2 large stalks celery, cut in chunks
- 2 large onions, cut in thick slabs
- 3 whole cloves garlic, peeled
- 2 tablespoons tomato paste
  Handful fresh parsley sprigs
- 1 teaspoon whole peppercorns
- ½ teaspoon dried mustard
- 2 10-ounce cans beef broth (Canned beef broth also tastes much better than the bouillon-cube broth.)
- 2 cups water
- ½ cup dry red wine or dry sherry

Proceed as for Chicken Gravy. Do *not* add baby formula.

Makes 2 ½ cups gravy.

Guacamole

LET ME DISPEL one misconception right away. Burying an avocado pit inside a bowl of guacamole does not keep the guacamole from turning brown. The two things that help avocado keep its color are citric acid, which is found in the lime juice we put in guacamole, and lack of air, which is found under very tight plastic wrap.

I keep expecting guacamole to vanish from the culture, but it keeps hanging on. In fact, it's improved from the days when it had to be completely smooth and ungarlicky, like pea soup. Now it's okay to serve people guacamole that's a little scary.

2	large cloves garlic, chopped
1	jalapeño pepper, seeded and chopped
3	ripe avocados, halved, peeled and pitted (And remember—you don't have to save the pits.)
¼	cup fresh lime juice (add more to taste)
1	large tomato, seeded and chopped
1	small red onion, minced
2	scallions, chopped fine
2	tablespoons fresh cilantro, chopped fine
2	teaspoons ground cumin
1	teaspoon fresh-ground black pepper
	Salt to taste

Turn on your food processor and drop the garlic and jalapeño in while the machine is running. Leave it running until they're as fine as possible.

Add 1 of the avocados and the lime juice. Process the mixture until it's completely smooth. Scrape the puree out into a medium bowl.

Add the other 2 avocados and mash them coarsely with a fork. Stir in the tomato, onions, scallions, cilantro, cumin, pepper and salt to taste and mix thoroughly. Cover the guacamole tightly with plastic wrap, let it sit at room temperature for 1 hour and haul in that wheelbarrow of tortilla chips.

Makes about 6 cups; serves 4.

Ice Cream in General

I T'S NOT EASY to come up with the best homemade ice creams when one superpremium store-bought brand is better than practically anything you can make. (You know the one I mean.) I know that both my parents and my parents-in-law would disagree with me about this. My parents-in-law think that brand is "too icy," and my parents think it's too rich. Once, when I held a blind taste test of vanilla ice creams, my parents *still* thought that brand was too rich.

Anyway, no point in getting worked up about that. The point is, that brand is hard to beat. Here are a few recipes that are either richer or something that brand doesn't yet offer. (When they start selling blueberry ice cream, I think I'll just give up.)

All these recipes need an ice-cream maker, either electric or manual. I'm not one of those people who insists on using a manual machine. They're maddeningly hard to churn. People always joke about how you at least work off some of the ice cream's calories in advance, but I bet you don't work off a tenth of what you're about to eat; you don't get any aerobic benefits; and the ice cream doesn't come out any better, either.

Electric ice-cream makers are good things to have, though. I gave my husband one of those expensive counter-top deals for his birthday about ten years ago. (It was on sale. Of course I was really giving it to myself.) Although a sign on the top of the machine warns you not to turn the machine on its side "even for few seconds," it's quite durable and has churned out quart after quart without any trouble. The only problem is cleaning it up. You can't lift out the ice-cream-churning bowl to clean it; you have to pour warm water into the bowl and dab at it with paper towels. I guess that's why the machine was on sale.

(See also individual entries for Blueberry Ice Cream, Chocolate Ice Cream, Coffee Ice Cream, Grape Ice Cream and Vanilla Ice Cream.)

Kimchi (Korean Pickled Cabbage)

NOT THAT ANYONE ASKED. I just felt like it. There aren't a lot of foods that start with K.

         1   head Chinese celery cabbage
         3   tablespoons (*yes, 3*) salt
         2   cups cold water
         1   teaspoon all-purpose flour
         ½   cup boiling water
         ½   cup daikon (Japanese white radish), peeled and julienned
         2   scallions, cut into 1-inch pieces
         1   tablespoon finely minced garlic
      1 ½   teaspoons sugar
      1 ½   teaspoons peeled, finely minced fresh ginger
         1   teaspoon dried hot chili peppers, finely ground (If you grind them in a food processor, don't lean your face over the top.)

Cut the cabbage crosswise through the center section. You'll only be using the bottom half, so do what you want with the top.

Put the bottom half of the cabbage in a small glass or stainless-steel bowl. Sprinkle 2 tablespoons of the salt between the leaves. Pour the cold water over the cabbage and let the mixture rest overnight at room temperature.

Rinse the cabbage completely, in several changes of water. Drain it well. Then place it in a clean dish towel and squeeze out the excess liquid.

Stir the flour into the boiling water until the mixture is smooth.

Combine the daikon, scallions, garlic, sugar, ginger, 1½ teaspoons salt and ground chili pepper. Stir in half of the flour mixture and blend well.

Fold back the leaves of the cabbage and spread equal portions of the spice mixture onto each leaf. (Don't pull the leaves off the core.) Rub the rest of the spice mixture over the outside of the cabbage.

Put the cabbage into a wide-mouth 2-cup glass jar that will hold it tightly. Add the remaining 1½ teaspoons of salt to the rest of the flour-and-water mixture, and pour this liquid over the cabbage.

Cover the jar tightly. Allow the mixture to marinate at room temperature for 2 days. Then take out the cabbage, cut off any tough stems, and slice the rest of the cabbage crosswise into 1-inch sections.

Serve as a side dish or condiment, being sure to warn timid elderly people that the recipe is very hot. Store in the refrigerator.

Makes 2 cups.

Lemon Squares

FIRST, START WITH LIMES. You can still call these lemon squares, of course. No one will put you in jail. People will just wonder why your lemon squares are so much more interesting than theirs.

Second, put in more juice and rind than any other recipe calls for. Once you've tasted lemon squares that are really lemony, the rest will all taste like vanilla pudding to you.

If you have some citrus salt, you can add a pinch of that too. Citrus salt is an extract of lemons and limes. It's used in Middle Eastern cooking and available in Middle Eastern stores. It's not salty: it's so sour that tasting even a few grains makes your ears hurt. Generally, it is mixed with water and substituted for lemon juice, but it can also be used to sour a recipe straight up.

Crust
- 1   **cup all-purpose flour**
- ½   **cup (1 stick) chilled unsalted butter, cut into ½-inch slices**
- 2   **tablespoons sugar**
- 1-2   **tablespoons almond paste**
- 2   **teaspoons grated lime rind**
-       **Pinch salt**

Filling
- 1   **cup sugar, stirred together with 1 tablespoon plus 1 teaspoon cornstarch**
- ½   **cup fresh-squeezed lime juice**
- 2   **large eggs**
- 1   **tablespoon grated lime rind**
- ½   **teaspoon baking powder**
- ¼   **teaspoon citrus salt (optional)**

Confectioners' sugar for dusting the top

Crust: Preheat the oven to 375 degrees F. Butter an 8-inch-square baking pan.

Place all the crust ingredients into the bowl of a food processor. Process until the mixture just begins to form a ball. Then pat the mixture into the greased pan and bake for 15 to 20 minutes, or until it is a pale golden all over. Turn the oven down to 350 degrees.

Filling: Wipe out the food processor with a paper towel and place all the filling ingredients into the bowl. Process until very smooth, about 1 minute. Pour into the partially baked crust and bake for 20 minutes.

Cool, then chill well. Cover with a light dusting of confectioners' sugar and cut into squares. Serve them cold. (My mother-in-law once tried to keep herself from eating some lemon squares she wanted to save. She wrapped them up and put them into the freezer. Then she discovered how much better lemon squares taste when they're frozen.)

Makes 16.

Lemonade

I PASS ALONG THIS RECIPE knowing you probably won't use it. The Minute Maid concentrate is pretty good, after all, and lemonade may not be as important to you as it is to me. But you might want to try making a batch of homemade if only to be able to tell people about it. Also, the lemonade syrup keeps for a month in the refrigerator. It could come in handy for—I don't know—glazing a cake or something—and it would certainly perk up your o.j. in the morning.

8   large lemons
2   cups sugar
2   cups water

Soften the lemons by rolling them on a tabletop and then microwaving them on "high" for 1 minute, if you have a microwave. If not, no sweat. With the sharpest vegetable peeler you can dig up, remove the lemon zest from each lemon. Be careful not to peel off any of the gross white pith under the rind.

Combine the sugar and water in a medium saucepan over medium heat. Stir constantly until they reach a boil, at which point stop stirring and turn the heat down slightly. Add the lemon rind and cover the saucepan. Boil the syrup for 4 minutes. Then strain it, discarding the lemon rind. Cool the syrup thoroughly.

Juice the lemons, strain the juice into the syrup, and stir well. Store covered in the refrigerator.

When guests arrive, ask them, "Would you by any chance like a little HOME-MADE LEMONADE THAT I MADE MYSELF?" Naturally they will be unable to refuse. To turn the lemonade syrup into lemonade, mix 1 part of syrup with 2 parts cold water. Garnish each glass with a couple of fresh lemon slices. (Seltzer water goes well with this syrup, too, and is perhaps slightly more adult.)

This recipe makes 1 generous quart of syrup, which will produce 3 generous quarts of lemonade.

Papa Bear's Own Lentil Soup

MY FRIEND Cindy Kane sent me this recipe, which she discovered in the manuscript of an Italian cookbook her husband Harry was illustrating. I've replaced some of the water in the original recipe with chicken stock, but that's the only change I've made. To keep the recipe entirely vegetarian, you could use vegetable stock instead.

The cookbook's author, Father Orsini, introduces the soup thus: "*Resuscitare i morti*, which means, 'This dish would bring back the dead!' Of course we know that the dead will rise again, not due to this soup, as delicious as it is, but because of the power of Jesus' Resurrection."

1	quart chicken stock
1	quart water
1	pound dried lentils, washed and picked over
2	medium potatoes, peeled and diced
2	medium onions, diced
2	large tomatoes, peeled, seeded and quartered
2	large carrots, peeled and diced
3	cloves garlic, minced
1	teaspoon dried oregano
½	teaspoon fresh-ground black pepper
½	cup olive oil
	Salt to taste

In a large pot, bring the chicken stock and water to a boil. Add all the other ingredients at once.

Bring the soup to a boil and allow it to continue boiling for 15 minutes. Then simmer it over low heat for ½ hour. Done!

Cindy's letter ended, "It really is the best lentil soup you EVER tasted—and it gets better the second and third nights."

Serves 6.

Lime Quick Bread

As with my recipe for Lemon Squares, this started out as lemon bread and got gentrified along the way. It's not that I don't like lemons; it's just that they don't have the same cachet as limes. (Lemons are the old friends you left at home when you moved to the city; limes are your new best friends.) Since juicing limes takes a little more work, lime dishes seem more appropriate for company. Also, I like the pleasantly scary look of a green-flecked baked good.

Bread

3	cups cake flour
1	tablespoon baking powder
½	teaspoon salt
½	cup (1 stick) unsalted butter, at room temperature
1	cup sugar
2	large eggs
1	cup less 2 tablespoons milk
2	tablespoons fresh lime juice (Don't put the lime juice into the milk or the milk will curdle. This won't really affect the bread, but it will look sickening.)
1	tablespoon grated lime rind

Glaze

¼	cup fresh lime juice
¼	cup sugar (preferably superfine)

Bread: Preheat the oven to 350 degrees F. Butter and flour a 9- x-5-inch loaf pan.

Into a medium bowl, sift together the flour, baking powder and salt. Set them aside.

Cream the butter and sugar until light. Add the eggs, one at a time. Then beat in the milk, the lime juice and the lime rind. Add the dry ingredients and mix only until they're combined. (I never know what cookbooks mean when they say that. I guess they don't want you to go on blindly beating and beating the batter. But why would you?)

Pour the batter into the prepared loaf pan and bake for 60 to 70 minutes, or until a tester inserted in the middle of the bread comes out clean. Meanwhile, make the glaze.

Glaze: Stir together the glaze ingredients until the sugar is dissolved. If you think of it, give it a stir occasionally while the bread is baking, so the sugar won't settle out.

The moment the bread is done, without taking it out of the pan, poke holes in it with a skewer and pour the lime glaze over the top.

Cool the bread for ½ hour. Then carefully invert it onto a rack, remove the pan and turn it right-side up to finish cooling. Serve the bread the same day you make it. It doesn't freeze well.

Makes one 9-x-5-inch loaf.

Lime Sorbet Supreme

I KEEP THINKING I should branch out into more kinds of sorbet, but I never get tired of this one. Once, when he was making a batch, my husband offered a taste to a friend of ours. "What do you think?" my husband asked. "There's not enough," the friend replied.

We always keep a batch of simple syrup in the refrigerator just in case we feel like making this. Once I accidentally poured some for a friend instead of water. She, thinking it was some kind of hideous diet soda, sipped it politely and didn't say anything. Now we keep the syrup bottle labeled.

You'll need an ice-cream maker for this.

Simple Syrup
- 3   **cups sugar**
- 3   **cups water**

Lime Sorbet
- 2 ½   **cups thoroughly chilled simple syrup**
- 1 ¼   **cups fresh lime juice**
- 2   **tablespoons finely grated lime rind**

Simple syrup: In a large saucepan, over high heat, bring the sugar and water to a boil. Lower the heat and continue boiling the syrup for 5 minutes. Cool and chill it.

Lime sorbet: Mix all the ingredients together, pour them into your ice-cream maker and freeze according to the manufacturer's directions. It's best served immediately.

Makes 1 quart. Unless you're serving some to my husband, serve small portions at first. The flavor is so intense that people tend to eat the sorbet in very small bites.

The Most Humane Way to Kill a Lobster

HORRIBLE THOUGHT! But you have to do it once in a while. I used to make my husband drop the lobsters into the boiling water until I decided that wasn't fair to him. Why should he have to kill all the lobsters in our house?

The first time I dropped the poor thing (the lobster, I mean) into the steaming pot, I inadvertently shrieked out, "God have mercy!"

At least—thanks to Julia Child—I knew I was killing the lobsters the nicest way I could. With her typical energy, Mrs. Child actually contacted the U.S. Bureau of Fisheries and several marine biologists to find out once and for all what to do with her lobsters. From these authorities she learned the following:

> The lobster's blood, or life fluid, flows almost randomly through the body spaces. . . . Any large incision made in the shell allows the liquid to drain out (it forms a pale blue clot); the lobster then slowly suffocates because the main function of this fluid is to transport oxygen around to body tissues. Thus, plunging a knife between the eyes is slow suffocation, as is plunging a knife in the back where tail joins chest. This last is not only slow suffocation, but, worse, it severs the intestine, dumping its contents over the tail meat. [*Yuck!*] The only knife work that can be effective is plunging it in ½ inch across the underside, close to the chest; this severs the spinal cord and kills the lobster, as well as draining out its life fluid.

> Many humanitarians, including for a while the International Society for the Protection of Animals, have been under the delusion that setting lobsters in cold water and bringing them slowly to the boil was the kindest treatment. No! This, again, is slow suffocation—plus death by drowning.

The most humane way to deal with live lobsters is to plunge them head first and upside down into boiling water. Since their circulatory functions are centered at the back of the head, they die within a few seconds. Then, if you are to cut up the lobsters before proceeding to the cooking, remove them in about a minute, when limp. Otherwise continue to boil them for the amount of time specified in the recipe.

I don't really think I can add anything to that.

Lobster Salad

Y OU SHOULDN'T TINKER with lobster salad too much, unless you're so rich that you want people to know you can afford to squander lobster by serving it in unlikeable ways. This recipe doesn't drown the main ingredient in toasted almonds and currants and chopped pickles. The lobster has center stage. The things I've added are simply enhancements.

This recipe calls for crème fraîche. This slightly soured heavy cream can be found in some supermarkets in the dairy section, or it can be made at home: Combine 1 cup of heavy cream with ½ cup of sour cream in a small bowl. Cover the bowl and let it stand at room temperature for 8 to 24 hours, until the mixture has thickened. Chill the crème fraîche for several hours before using. It will keep in the refrigerator for 2 weeks.

1	2-pound lobster (or two 1-pound lobsters), cooked and cooled
1 ¼	cups watercress leaves
3	tablespoons crème fraîche
3	tablespoons mayonnaise
1	tablespoon dry white wine
1	tablespoon fresh lemon juice
1	tablespoon minced fresh chives
1	tablespoon finely minced fresh tarragon
	Salt and fresh-ground black pepper

Take the lobster apart in whatever way works best for you. (A very good way is to have someone else do it.) Dice the lobster meat and put it into your serving bowl with the watercress. Chill.

In a small bowl, fold together everything else except the salt and pepper. Gently combine the dressing with the lobster and the watercress. Add salt and pepper to taste, and more lemon juice or chives if you think they're needed. Chill the salad for ½ hour before serving.

Serves 2.

Company Meat Loaf

Cookbook authors must battle with the constant temptation to steal other cookbook authors' recipes. It's not considered stealing if you make three major changes in the recipe. (Major means you can't add another quarter-teaspoon of salt; you must add an entire cup.) You're on the honor system. Make those three changes, and the recipe now belongs to you, or so the theory goes.

Sometimes, though, a recipe comes along that you want *intensely* to make your own—and yet the recipe is perfect as is. This meat loaf, from **The Silver Palate Good Times Cookbook** (where it's called Italian Meat Loaf), is such a recipe. I've changed a couple of ditsy things. I add less liquid, and the spices I use are a little different. I've changed the cheese from mozzarella to Swiss: we often eat this meat loaf cold, and cold baked mozzarella is more plasticky than cheesy. I've also changed the way the meat loaf is cooked. Instead of baking it, I smoke it in our Hasti-Bake. Although you should go and buy a Hasti-Bake to get the best effect, a gas grill with a cover will work okay.

But this recipe really belongs to Julee Rosso and Sheila Lukins. Maybe one day I'll petition them to let me adopt it.

Note: You will need a generous amount of charcoal, enough to keep a wide surface of the grill hot for over 1 hour.

2	pounds ground beef chuck
1	pound sweet Italian sausage, casings removed (Try to have these and the beef at room temperature. Your hands can get very uncomfortable squishing through cold meat.)
1	medium-size yellow onion, chopped
5	cloves garlic, minced
3	cups fresh bread crumbs
1	cup chopped fresh Italian parsley
1	tablespoon dried oregano
1	tablespoon dried basil
1	teaspoon salt
½	teaspoon fresh-ground black pepper

2   large eggs, lightly beaten
½   cup dry red wine
2   cups fresh basil leaves
4   ounces sun-dried tomatoes (packed in oil), drained, dried with paper
    towels and chopped
1   pound Swiss cheese, grated

Fire up your grill. Line a 9-x-13-inch baking pan with aluminum foil.

In a large bowl, combine the ground beef, sausage, onion, garlic, bread crumbs, parsley, herbs and salt and pepper to taste. Add the eggs and wine and mix thoroughly.

Lay out one large sheet of parchment paper or plastic wrap. Spread the meat-loaf mixture out in a 15-x-12-inch rectangle on the paper. Arrange the basil leaves over the surface and cover them with the chopped dried tomatoes. On top of that, sprinkle three-quarters of the grated cheese.

Now comes the hard part. Using the paper or plastic wrap to move things along, roll the meat loaf up like a jelly roll. (Start from a short end.) Roll the loaf as tightly as you can, and keep peeling back the paper as you roll.

When you have achieved loafdom, pinch the meat-loaf seam closed as best you can. (This meat loaf has a tendency to ooze.) Then use the parchment or plastic wrap to gently sling the meat loaf over to the foil-lined pan. Place it seam-side down in the pan. Now pinch the ends closed as best you can.

Place the pan on the grill rack and cover the grill, leaving the air holes at the top and bottom fully open. Cook for 1 hour. When the hour is up, scatter the rest of the cheese on top of the meat loaf. Cook it for 10 minutes longer.

Serve either hot or cold. Cold, it slices prettily—well, attractively. Let's not demand the impossible.

Serves 8.

"Cookbook authors must battle with the constant temptation to steal other cookbook authors' recipes."

Mom-Style Meat Loaf

WHENEVER I MAKE MEAT LOAF, I remember the "I Love Lucy" episode where Lucy loses her engagement ring making meat loaf. Ricky says, "Don't cry, honey. I'll get you a new ring with big diamonds all the way around," and Lucy sobs back, "No! I want my old ring with little diamonds *halfway* around!"

This recipe—authentically Mom-ish, but quite delicious—comes from Joan and Eric Brown, who are also the architects of the Plum Pudding on page 155.

1	pound ground sirloin
½	pound hot Italian sausage, casings removed
1	8-ounce can whole tomatoes, drained and chopped
¼	pound mushrooms, sliced and sautéed in 1-2 tablespoons butter until they give up their liquid
½	cup minced onion
¼	cup Worcestershire sauce
¼	cup Dijon mustard
2	large eggs, well beaten
2	tablespoons dried oregano
1	teaspoon fresh-ground black pepper
½	teaspoon salt

Preheat the oven to 350 degrees F.

Mix all the ingredients thoroughly by hand. Press the mixture into a 9-x-5-inch loaf pan.

Bake the meat loaf for 1 ½ hours, draining excess fat halfway through the baking.

Serves 6.

Grandma Joyce's Molasses Cookies

THIS WAS THE FIRST RECIPE I ever made all by myself, when I was eight or nine. And it was all by myself that I put in 2 cups of molasses instead of ½ cup. My mother, who had tactfully retired upstairs, called down, "Those smell very good, honey! OH! THEY SMELL TOO GOOD! THEY'RE BURNING!" She galloped down the stairs and helped me pull the cookies out of the oven, except that they weren't cookies any longer. They were a bubbling sheet of molasses tar. Well, it was one way to get the difference between ½ and 2 fixed in my mind.

1 ½	cups (3 sticks) unsalted butter, at room temperature
2	cups sugar
2	large eggs
½	cup "light" or "medium"-flavored molasses
4	cups all-purpose flour
4	teaspoons baking soda
½	teaspoon salt
2	teaspoons cinnamon
2	teaspoons ginger
1	teaspoon cloves
	Demerara or other large-crystalled sugar

In a large bowl, cream the butter and sugar. Add the eggs and molasses and blend well. In a separate bowl, sift together the flour, baking soda, salt and spices; beat into the molasses mixture. Cover the mixture with plastic wrap and chill it for 1 hour.

Fifteen minutes before the chilling time is up, preheat the oven to 375 degrees F.

Line your cookie sheets with parchment paper. Roll the dough into walnut-sized balls and dip each ball in the sugar. Place 3 inches apart on the cookie sheets.

Bake for 10 to 12 minutes, or until the outsides of the cookies are crackly-looking and the insides are still soft. It's easiest just to slide the parchment paper right off the sheets onto your kitchen counters, but you can also transfer the cookies to racks and reuse the parchment.

Makes 5 dozen.

Fried Mushrooms

I DON'T MEAN FRIED *breaded* mushrooms. You'll have to get that recipe from Denny's or Friendly's or something. (I wonder how many people think, "Well, there's my vegetable for the day" when they eat that kind of fried mushrooms.) I mean the kind of mushrooms you sauté to go along with steak.

This is Nora Ephron's technique. She didn't give it to me; I read about it in **Heartburn**. What you have to do is use a large skillet, get the butter very hot and sauté the sliced mushrooms or mushroom caps a few at a time so that their little gray sides don't touch. Overcrowding will ruin them.

You also have to be patient and fry the mushrooms till they're a nice burnished mahogany. Keep the ones you've already fried in a warm oven so you won't sneak them all before it's time to serve them.

Incidentally, if you're ever sautéing mushrooms and onions together—and you surely will be for some recipe or other—a pinch of thyme is a compulsory addition.

"You'll have to get the recipe for fried *breaded* mushrooms from Denny's or Friendly's or something."

Oatmeal Bread

I THINK QUICK ROLLED OATS ARE SISSIES, except possibly in this recipe. If you want to use them at the end of the process—the part where you work in ¾ cup to give the bread an oatier texture—that's fine with me. But *only* for that part.

Bread
- 1 ½ cups old-fashioned rolled oats, plus ¾ cup more for kneading in later
- 2 cups half-and-half
- 5 tablespoons unsalted butter
- ½ cup light brown sugar, packed
- 2 teaspoons salt
- ½ cup lukewarm water
- 1 package active dry yeast
- 1 teaspoon sugar
- ¼ teaspoon ginger
- 4 ½ cups bread flour or all-purpose flour
- Pinch mace

Glaze
- 1 tablespoon milk
- 1 tablespoon honey
- 1 egg yolk

Bread: Place the 1 ½ cups oats in a large bowl. (If you have an electric mixer with a dough hook, put them in the mixer bowl.) Rinse a small saucepan with cold water before you pour in the half-and-half; this will make for easier cleanup later. Heat the half-and-half to scalding and pour it over the oats. Add the butter, brown sugar and salt. Stir until the butter has melted; then let the mixture stand until it's cool. If you're in a hurry, you can put the bowl into a pan of ice water.

Once the oatmeal mixture has cooled, pour the lukewarm water into a small bowl. Stir in the yeast, sugar and the ginger. Let the mixture proof for 10 minutes, or until bubbly.

Pour the yeast mixture into the oat mixture and stir well. Then stir in the flour, the additional ¾ cup of rolled oats and the mace. Knead for 5 minutes, either by hand or with a dough hook, until the dough is elastic and not as sticky as it was before. It will still be sticky, though.

Place the dough into a buttered bowl, cover it, and let it rise until doubled in bulk. This first rising takes longer than is usual in breads—often several hours. I sometimes make the dough before I go to bed and leave it overnight in a cold part of my house. Not the refrigerator, just in some drafty uninsulated spot. There are lots of them in my house.

When the dough has doubled, punch it down. Divide it into two parts, shape them into loaves as best you can (buttering your hands may help) and place them into buttered 8-x-4-inch loaf pans. Cover the pans with a damp towel and let the dough rise until doubled in bulk. This time it will take a couple of hours at the most.

Preheat the oven to 375 degrees F.

Glaze: Beat the glaze ingredients together.

When the loaves have risen, brush them with the glaze. Then bake them for 45 minutes, or until the bottoms of the loaves sound hollow when thumped. Turn them out of the pans onto a rack and let them cool.

Makes two 8-x-4-inch loaves.

Onion Rings

I HATE the kind of onion ring where your first bite pulls a long, slimy string of onion right out of the coating, leaving a hollow ring of fry with nothing inside. I also hate the kind where the onion is pale-blue and boiled-tasting. And I hate the kind with soft, puffy batter surrounding a tiny little fleck of onion. Who wants an onion fritter?

But I can hear you muttering, *If you can't say something nice, don't say anything at all*. While that attitude is alien to me, I can certainly say something nice about *my* kind of onion rings. I like the onion to be browned as well as the coating. (They're supposed to be french-fried onion rings, not French-fried breading.) I like a thin, crisp, barely-dusted-on coating with lots of pepper, and I like bits of browned onion poking out here and there. And I like them to be much saltier than is healthy.

And now I can hear you saying *I, I, I. Is "I" the only word you know?* No. I also know the words "You'll definitely need a frying or candy thermometer for this recipe."

Note: Deep-frying is not without its hazards. (Besides health hazards, I mean.) If you're not familiar with the process, it would be a good idea to read through the directions in **Joy of Cooking** or some similar tome.

3	**cups milk**
1	**large egg**
4	**large Spanish onions, cut into ½-inch slices and separated into rings (Don't worry if some of the rings break apart.)**
	Approximately 2 quarts corn oil
1½	**cups all-purpose flour**
1½	**cups yellow cornmeal**
1	**tablespoon fresh-ground black pepper**
2	**teaspoons salt**
	Pinch cayenne (optional)

Beat the milk and the egg together. Pour them into a 9-x-13-inch pan and layer the onion rings evenly in the pan. Let the rings soak for 1 hour, turning occasionally.

Into a deep fryer or large, heavy saucepan, pour enough corn oil to come to a depth of 3 inches. Preheat the oil to 375 degrees F. Be patient with this. The onion rings will taste gross if they're fried at too low a heat.

As the oil heats, dump the flour, cornmeal, pepper, salt and optional cayenne into a large plastic bag or brown-paper shopping bag. Shake the dry ingredients a few times to blend. Take the onions out of their milk bath and shake them in the flour mix until they're thoroughly coated.

Preheat the oven to 200 degrees.

A few at a time, take the onions out of the bag, shake off any excess coating and drop them carefully into the hot oil. Fry until they're well browned. Drain them on paper towels, salt them to taste and keep them warm in the oven. Repeat the process until all the onions have been fried.

Serve immediately.

When the oil cools, you can strain and reuse it a couple more times. But do you really want to? I'd get rid of it, myself.

Serves 4 to 6.

"I hate the kind of onion ring where your first bite pulls a long, slimy string of onion right out of the coating."

Not-At-All-Classic Onion Soup

LET'S GET AWAY from the classic onion soup with its too-salty stock and soggy bread and strands of cheese flopping all over the place. Let's put the cheese right into the soup, as they did in the first **Moosewood Cookbook**. This soup is subtle, comforting and—you won't think this is a compliment, but it is—reminiscent of cheese fondue. When I noticed this resemblance, and realized to my embarrassment that I actually *missed* cheese fondue, I decided to heighten the soup's fondue-ishness a bit. If you don't harbor a yearning for fondue yourself, you could take out the kirsch. Oh, and put the fondue forks back down in the basement.

5	tablespoons unsalted butter
3	cups thinly sliced onions
2	large cloves garlic, minced
¾	teaspoon dry mustard
½	teaspoon salt (or more, depending on how salty the stock is)
1½	cups chicken stock
½	cup dry white wine
3	tablespoons all-purpose flour
1½	cups milk, warmed
1½	cups grated Emmenthaler cheese
2	tablespoons kirsch
½	teaspoon prepared white horseradish
	Salt and fresh-ground black pepper
1-2	"grates" of nutmeg

Heat 2 tablespoons of the butter in a medium saucepan. Add the onions, garlic, mustard and salt. Cook over low heat until the onions are translucent, about 15 to 20 minutes; don't let them or the garlic brown. This soup isn't supposed to taste brown.

Add the chicken stock and wine. Cover the pan and let it simmer over low heat.

Meanwhile, in another medium saucepan, over medium heat, melt the remaining 3 tablespoons of butter. Whisk in the flour all at once and cook it for 1 minute, whisking constantly. Then turn the heat way, way down and whisk in the milk. Cook this mixture, whisking constantly, until it makes a smooth, thick sauce. Add the cheese, kirsch and horseradish and whisk till combined.

Now you have a cheese sauce. You could use it to make a cheese soufflé, but that would get us off the track. Instead, add it to the onions and mix thoroughly. Add salt and pepper to taste, grate in a little nutmeg and cook the soup over low heat for 10 minutes. Stir it often. Then serve it.

Serves 3 to 4.

Creamed Onions For Our Time

MAYBE I'M THE LAST PERSON in the world to care about creamed onions, but damn it, I'm gonna get 'em *right*! And none of those floury white sauces, either. And no canned onions bobbling around in their jars like something preserved in formaldehyde. And no one else at the Thanksgiving table even noticing all the trouble I've gone to, but that's okay. As we snootily say to children, *All the more for me*.

- 3 pounds small pearl onions, parboiled in boiling water for 1 minute and peeled
- 3 tablespoons unsalted butter
- 1 teaspoon sugar
- ½ teaspoon salt
- 1 large clove garlic, minced
- ¾ cup heavy cream
  Salt and fresh-ground black pepper
- ⅔ cup minced fresh parsley

Butter the bottom and sides of a large, heavy skillet that's big enough to hold the onions in one layer. That done, put the onions in the skillet in one layer. Dot them with slices of the butter and sprinkle the sugar, salt and garlic over them.

Pour in enough water to come halfway up the sides of the onions. Bring the water to a boil and let it continue to boil until the liquid has mostly evaporated. Very, very gently, with a pancake turner, turn the onions over if they seem to be starting to stick. Stirring would make them fall apart. To "stir" the liquid in the skillet, swirl the skillet from time to time.

Continue to cook the onions until they are golden brown, deepening, in spots, to regular brown, about 10 minutes. Add the cream, bring it to a boil and cook it for a few seconds until it begins to thicken. Season to taste and stir in the parsley.

When you're making something in a pale-colored sauce, by the way, don't listen to the people who tell you you have to use white pepper. "If people see little black specks in the sauce, they won't know what they are," is the common reasoning. But of course they'll know what they are: they're pepper. Do any of your friends really think you'd serve food with visible bits of dead bug in it?

Happy Thanksgiving.

Serves 6.

Peach Pie

PEACH SOUP, a friend of mine once called it. This recipe is kind of, well, liquidy. But I prefer to think of the liquid as divine ichor rather than soup. Oops. I've just checked ichor in the dictionary. "The ethereal fluid flowing in the veins of the ancient Greek gods," it says. Well, that's close enough to what I thought; but the second definition is "the watery ooze of an abrasion, sore or wound." *Hmmmm.* Not quite yummy-sounding enough, perhaps? Let's say that I prefer to think of the liquid as divine *elixir*. And if I haven't spoiled your appetite yet, you should go right down to the kitchen and make this.

Peach pie and my strawberry pie (page 178) are the only pies I bake two at a time. My family of four eats one for dessert and the other for breakfast the next morning.

For this pie's crust, I use all butter. Taste matters more than flakiness here.

Crust
- 1½ cups all-purpose flour
- ¼ teaspoon salt
- ¾ cup (1½ sticks) unsalted butter, chilled and cut into very thin slices
- 3 tablespoons ice water

Filling
- 1 cup light brown sugar, packed
- ⅓ cup all-purpose flour
- ⅛ teaspoon freshly grated nutmeg
- Pinch salt
- ¼ cup (½ stick) unsalted butter, at room temperature
- 4 large fresh peaches

Crust: Preheat the oven to 375 degrees F.

In a medium bowl, toss the flour and salt together. Scatter in the slices of butter and cut them into the flour with a pastry blender until the mixture has the texture of coarse meal. Sprinkle the ice water over all and stir gently with a fork until the mixture comes together into a dough. (If you need another teaspoon or so of water, that's okay.) Press the ball of dough into a disk, wrap the disk in plastic wrap and chill it for ½ hour.

While the dough is chilling, prepare the filling.

Filling and assembly: Stir together the dry ingredients until thoroughly mixed. Cut in the butter.

Butter the bottom and sides of a 9-inch pie pan. On a floured rolling surface, roll out the dough until it forms a circle about 12 inches in diameter. Line the pie pan with the dough, being careful not to stretch it. Crimp the sides. Stick the pan back in the refrigerator for 15 minutes.

Butter the shiny side of a 14-inch square of aluminum foil. Place the foil, butter-side down, in the pastry-lined pie tin. Fill it with 2 cups of pie weights, raw rice or dried beans. Bake the shell on a cookie sheet for 20 minutes. Meanwhile, peel the peaches. Pit them. Slice them.

Transfer the pie shell to a rack and remove the pie weights and foil. Turn the oven down to 350 degrees. Cool the pie shell for 10 minutes. Then spread half the brown-sugar-butter filling around the bottom and sides of the shell. Working quickly, arrange the peach slices in the shell and top with the remaining brown-sugar-butter filling.

Bake the pie on a cookie sheet for 40 to 50 minutes, until well browned on top. Allow it to cool slightly before cutting, but don't expect neat slices. The elixir, you know.

Makes one 9-inch pie.

"Let's say that I prefer to think of the liquid in this pie as divine elixir."

145

Neen's Peanut Sauce

MY SISTER CORNELIA devised this recipe, which I would cheerfully eat on slices of two-by-four. You can use this sauce for anything: a salad dressing (make sure the salad has lots of cucumbers), a cold-noodle dressing, a dip for raw vegetables, a glaze for barbecued chicken . . .

2	tablespoons corn oil
½	cup minced onion
2	cloves garlic, minced
1	tablespoon crushed red-pepper flakes
1	teaspoon ground cumin
¼	cup soy sauce
3	tablespoons fresh lime juice
1 ½	cups smooth peanut butter
¾	cup unsweetened canned coconut milk

Heat the oil in a skillet. Over low heat, sauté the onion, garlic, red-pepper flakes and cumin for 10 minutes. Don't let the onion or garlic get brown.

Stir in the soy sauce and lime juice. Gradually stir in 1 cup of the peanut butter and ½ cup of the coconut milk. Stirring constantly, cook the mixture over low heat for 5 minutes.

Take the stuff off the heat and spoon it into a mixing bowl. Let it cool. Then, with an electric mixer, beat in the remaining ½ cup of peanut butter and the remaining ¼ cup of coconut milk. Continue to beat until the mixture is quite smooth and the color of peanut butter once again.

Makes 2 ½ cups.

Pecan Pie

I WOULD LIKE TO DEDICATE this recipe to my brother, who likes pecan pie so much that he even buys those tiny industrial pecan pies they sell near the cash register at 7-Eleven.

Two hazards lurk in wait for pecan-pie makers. The first is soggy pecans that sludge between your teeth like bits of cheese. The second is too much sugar. Not that the sugar in a pecan pie always takes the form of *sugar*. Sometimes it takes the form of dark corn syrup uncut with anything except melted butter. The majority of homemade pecan pies would be twice as good if they were half as sweet.

So. We get rid of the dark corn syrup. We toast the pecans a little. We produce an exceptional dessert halfway between a pie and a tart, and then what? I guess we have no choice but to market a mass-produced individual version at 7-Eleven.

Crust
- 1 ¼ cups all-purpose flour
- ¼ tcaspoon salt
- ½ cup (1 stick) plus 2 tablespoons unsalted butter, chilled and cut into thin slices
- 2 ½ tablespoons ice water, plus a little more if necessary

Filling
- ½ cup (1 stick) unsalted butter
- ½ cup Lyle's Golden Syrup (You can buy this at specialty stores and many supermarkets in thc honcy-and-molasses section, or substitute ¼ cup dark corn syrup plus ¼ cup light corn syrup.)
- ⅓ cup heavy cream
- ½ cup light brown sugar, packed
- ⅛ teaspoon salt
- 2 ½ cups shelled pecans, coarsely chopped and toasted for 5 minutes at 350 degrees (You can do this while the crust is baking.)
- Whipped cream for topping

Crust: In a medium bowl, stir together the flour and the salt. Drop the slices of butter over the flour's surface and cut them in according to your favorite pie-crust-cutting-in method; I use a pastry blender myself. When the mixture has the texture of coarse meal, stir in the water with a fork, adding a few more droplets if necessary to make the mixture adhere. Press the dough into a disk-shape, wrap it in plastic wrap and chill it for ½ hour.

Butter a 9-inch pie tin.

On a floured surface, roll out the dough into a circle about 12 inches in diameter. Fit the dough into the pie tin without stretching it anywhere. Tuck it down, trim and crimp the edges; and stick the pie tin into the refrigerator for 15 more minutes.

Preheat the oven to 350 degrees F.

Butter the shiny side of a 14-inch-square piece of foil. Fit the foil, buttered-side down, into the pie shell. With a fork, prick through the foil and the crust in several places. Then fill the foil with 2 cups of pie weights, raw rice or dried beans.

Bake the pie shell in the lower third of the oven for 15 minutes. Carefully lift out the foil and its contents and bake the naked shell for 5 more minutes. Cool the shell on a rack, but don't turn off the oven. You still need to bake the filling, don't forget.

Filling: In a medium saucepan, over medium heat, stir together the butter, Golden Syrup, cream, brown sugar and salt until the butter is melted and the sugar has dissolved. Remove from the heat. Cool well, then stir in the pecans until they are well coated.

Turn the filling into the pie shell. Bake in the lower third of the oven for 20 minutes. Then shift it to the middle of the oven and bake for 20 to 30 more minutes, or until the pie is well glazed and browned.

"Two hazards lurk in wait for pecan-pie makers."

Cool on a rack. Serve with whipped cream.

Makes one 9-inch pie.

Pecan Puffs, Mexican Wedding Cakes, Russian Teacakes

I KNOW YOU already have some version of this recipe, but the mace makes the difference. People eat these like popcorn.

- ½ cup (1 stick) unsalted butter, at room temperature
- 2 tablespoons sugar
- 1 cup pecans
- 1 cup all-purpose flour
  Pinch salt
- ½ teaspoon mace
- 1 teaspoon vanilla extract
  Confectioners' sugar

Preheat the oven to 300 degrees F.

Cream the butter and sugar together until the mixture is light. In a food processor, grind the pecans, flour and salt. Beat the pecan-flour mixture into the butter mixture. Beat in the mace and vanilla.

Roll the dough into small walnut-sized balls and place on ungreased cookie sheets. Bake the cookies for 30 minutes.

As you take the cookies out of the oven, roll them in a pan filled with confectioners' sugar. Cool the cookies on racks, then roll them in the confectioners' sugar once again.

Makes 20 cookies.

Pesto Torta
(Best Cocktail-Party Cheese Thing)

PESTO SHOULD BE AS DEVALUED as kiwi by now, but it's proving very durable. (So is kiwi, come to think of it.) Maybe there are some foods (kiwi is not one of them) that taste so good they simply aren't allowed to go out of style.

Up until now, I've been very babyish whenever people have asked for the recipe—which happened every time I served it. I reluctantly gave out the recipe a few times, then suddenly stopped. And I actually had a screaming argument (I was the one screaming) with my friend Martha about whether she had the right to make this torta for people I knew. I wanted to be the only person associated with the recipe. The worst thing is that even though I *know* I was wrong, I feel so proprietary about the recipe that I still secretly think I was right.

This is a dumb attitude, considering that I got the recipe out of a cookbook myself. **Beyond Parsley**, the book is called. It's a Kansas City Junior League cookbook and one of the best Junior League cookbooks I've ever seen. (Although it does have one very strange recipe for sausage cake iced with hard sauce.) I figured no one in my town would ever come across the book, so the recipe was as good as mine.

Now it's yours (but, really, still mine), and I apologize to one and all.

A 6-inch springform pan works best for this recipe, although you can also use any pan or mold that's about 6 inches in diameter.

2	8-ounce packages cream cheese, at room temperature
1	pound (4 sticks) unsalted butter, plus 2 tablespoons, at room temperature
2	ounces sun-dried tomatoes (dry-packed, not preserved in oil)
2	cups fresh basil leaves, tightly packed
½	cup fresh parsley
⅓	cup pine nuts, lightly toasted and cooled
2	cloves garlic
¼	teaspoon salt

½   cup olive oil
¾   cup freshly grated Parmesan

With an electric mixer, beat the cream cheese and the 1 pound butter together until smooth and creamy. Divide it into 6 equal portions.

Soak the dried tomatoes in warm water for 20 minutes. Drain them in a sieve and then dry them on paper towels. Cut them into small pieces.

In a food processor, process the basil, parsley, pine nuts, garlic and salt. Add the olive oil and process for 20 seconds. Scrape down the sides of the bowl. Add the Parmesan and the remaining 2 tablespoons butter and pulse the machine a few times until blended. Let the mixture drain in a sieve for at least ½ hour before using; it should be as dry as possible.

Cut an 18-inch square of cheesecloth. Moisten it with water, wring it dry, and smoothly line the springform pan with it, draping the excess over the rim of the pan.

Now take a rubber spatula and spread ⅙ of the cream-cheese mixture in the bottom of the lined pan. "Frost" the cream-cheese mixture with ¼ of the drained pesto, making sure the pesto makes it all the way to the sides of the pan. Top the pesto with another sixth of the cream-cheese. On top of that layer, scatter half the dried-tomato bits, once again making sure that they reach the sides of the pan. (The different layers need to show when the torta is unmolded.) Cover them with another layer of cream cheese and butter. Repeat this messy but worth-it process until the pan is filled; the last, top layer should be cheese. If your pan or mold is wider than 6 inches, you can make fewer layers.

Tuck the ends of the cheesecloth up around the torta and gently press them down to compact the mixture slightly. Chill the torta overnight.

An hour before you plan to serve the torta, release it from the springform pan and gently unwrap it. (If you've used another pan or mold, invert it onto a serving dish and gently remove it from the mold. Then unwrap it.) Dig up a serving dish and put the torta on it.

If you want, you can decorate the top of the torta with more snipped-up dried tomatoes. I always stick a sprig of pachysandra in the top and jab a few more sprigs in around the base; you can do the same thing with holly at Christmas.

You can freeze the torta, still in its pan, in plastic wrap and a tightly sealed plastic bag. It will keep for 2 months. Thaw it in the refrigerator overnight.

"Pesto should be as devalued as kiwi by now, but it's proving very durable."

Serve with assorted crackers, and be prepared with some kind of lie when people ask you what kind of cheese you've used. No one wants to hear that they're eating equal parts of butter and cream cheese. Just tell them it's mascarpone cheese.

Makes one 6-inch torta, enough to serve 10 to 12.

Edible Playdough

NOT SOMETHING *you* would eat perhaps, but well worth messing up your kitchen counters with when it's a rainy day and your children are throttling each other. And it doesn't require a trip to the store, unless you're out of dried milk. Which you shouldn't be, because you should always keep some in your closet in case there's an earthquake or something and your power goes out for several days. Of course if that happened at my house, our water would stop too, and we always use up the bottled water I try to save for emergencies, and I can't see myself convincing the kids to try powdered milk *dry*. But I always keep a few envelopes of dried milk around anyway.

> 2   **cups smooth peanut butter**
> 2   **cups rolled oats**
> 2   **cups dried milk**
> ⅔   **cup honey**

Optional
> **Rice Krispies, coconut, sprinkles, chocolate chips, red hots, little olives, cocktail onions or other kid-pleasing garnishes**

Get your kids to mix all the ingredients until thoroughly combined. Then get them to wash their hands while you cover the whole kitchen with wax paper to make a work surface for them. Then give them the bowl of playdough and beat a hasty retreat.

You may want to pass out toothpicks so your kids can attach different sections of dough together or poke eyes into the faces of their blobby little creations. Make sure no one swallows a toothpick along with the dough. Store in an airtight container.

Makes 6 cups.

Super Playdough

THIS IS THE LEAST CRUMBLY and easiest to handle of all homemade playdoughs, and the Kool-Aid makes the dough smell less horrible. (Until I started making playdough for my kids, I never realized what salt smelled like.) Leave the Kool-Aid out, though, if you're working with kids who are so young they might actually try to eat dough with Kool-Aid in it. Although actually if they're young enough to try to eat it, they're going to try to eat it without Kool-Aid too.

Okay. Don't let kids under three near this recipe.

- 2 cups all-purpose flour
- ½ cup salt
- 2 packages *un*sweetened Kool-Aid
- 4 teaspoons cream of tartar
- 2 cups water
- 2 tablespoons corn oil

Mix all the ingredients together in a large saucepan. (My copy of the recipe says "in an electric skillet," but I don't have one.) Cook and stir over low heat until the mixture thickens and the bottom is just starting to crust up, about 15 minutes. The dough will be very stiff and hard to stir at this point.

Turn the dough out onto a large cookie sheet and allow it to cool. When cool, knead it until smooth. Store in a covered container.

Makes 3 cups.

Majestic Imperial Regal Yuletide Plum Pudding

THIS IS A TRUE BRITISH RECIPE, although it comes to me via Ohio, where Joan and Eric Brown make jillions of these to give away every year. In most plum puddings, "plum" seems to mean "large chunks of citron," but this one is blessedly citron-free. It's also much moister than most plum puddings. For me, the official end of Christmas comes when there's no more of this plum pudding left for breakfast.

You'll need a kitchen scale; as I said, this is a British recipe, and you know how they always weigh everything. The puddings should be made in October if you want to eat them at Christmas. Refrigerated, they last indefinitely, as long as you keep dousing them with brandy.

1	pound finely chopped beef suet (You can have the butcher do this, or do it yourself in a food processor.)
1	pound dark brown sugar, packed
1	pound regular raisins
1	pound golden raisins
1	pound chopped mixed peel (see "Peel," page 209)
1	pound whole-wheat bread crumbs (The crumbs should be homemade; the bread doesn't have to be.)
8	ounces dried currants
8	ounces dried cherries
4	ounces (1 cup) all-purpose flour
4	ounces chopped almonds
1	tablespoon cinnamon
2	teaspoons allspice
2	teaspoons cloves
2	teaspoons salt
1	teaspoon ginger
1	teaspoon cardamom
1	teaspoon freshly grated nutmeg
12	ounces Guinness Stout
1½	cups brandy
½	cup milk
8	*jumbo* eggs
	Juice and grated rind from 2 large lemons

In a large bowl, mix the suet, brown sugar, raisins, peel, bread crumbs, currants, cherries, flour, almonds and spices thoroughly by hand. Add all the liquids—the eggs should be added one at a time—and continue to hand-mix "until the mix becomes a true blend," as Eric writes. He adds, "One could use an electric mixer, I suppose, but that wouldn't be nearly as satisfying or as much fun. Traditionally, it is believed that to stir the pudding mix brings good luck in the new year. Mixing by hand guarantees that result."

Also—to drag us back to the practical—unless you have a very powerful mixer, you're going to overheat it in a second with a batter this heavy. And plum pudding batters have been known to snap spoons in half.

There will be about 2 gallons of batter, which you can distribute among your pudding bowls as you choose. Eric uses greased Pyrex bowls of varying sizes to steam his puddings; this recipe will fill six 12-ounce and two 24-ounce Pyrex bowls. You may need to use others, depending on your bowl supply; I've found that even custard cups work well if you're giving a tiny pudding to one person.

Spoon the batter into your bowls, molds or whatever. Cover the tops of the bowls tightly with, according to Eric, "a double layer of old sheet or other clean rag." Slightly dampened parchment paper works, too, and at my church—where we do plum puddings in quantity—we cover them with muslin bought for the purpose. Fasten the cloth or paper with a rubber band, then cover the puddings tightly with a layer of aluminum foil.

The next thing you need is a couple of large, lidded cooking vessels into which you can fit the pudding bowls as well as a rack to steam them on. A canning pot is perfect, or a big steamer or even a roasting pan if it can go on the stove. Place the racks inside the vessels, pour in enough water to provide steam without slopping up through the rack, and then arrange the puddings on the racks. Bring the water to a boil, and steam the puddings over low heat, checking the water levels frequently. The 12-ounce and 24-ounce sizes will take about 5 hours; smaller puddings will take a shorter time.

If you can't steam all the puddings at once, it's okay to do a second batch. In her Christmas book, Martha Stewart also suggests steaming large quantities of plum puddings in the oven. She puts her pudding bowls into large roasting pans, pours boiling water into the pans, covers the bowls and roasting pans with foil, and cooks everything in a preheated 300-degree-F oven for 5 hours, being sure to add boiling water as needed. I haven't tried this method, but I see no reason it wouldn't work.

When the puddings are done, remove them from the steamer and place them upside down on a wax-paper-covered surface. They will slide free of the bowls as they cool.

When the puddings are thoroughly cool, remove the foil and paper and place each inside a plastic bag along with 1 ounce of brandy. Seal the bag tightly, turn it over a couple of times to make sure it's not leaking, and store in the refrigerator until Christmas. Every 3 weeks, moisten the pudding with more brandy. When it's actually time to give the pudding away, place it in a new plastic bag, seal the bag tightly, and wrap it in foil. A bow is optional.

Whether you give some puddings away or keep them all for yourself, they should be brought to room temperature, unwrapped and steamed for another hour before serving. Serve them with hard sauce or with Mozart's Rum Sauce (recipe follows).

Makes six 12-ounce and two 24-ounce puddings.

Mozart's Rum Sauce (For Plum Pudding)

MOZART HIMSELF gave me this recipe. That's how it got its name. Once again I have to warn you that this contains uncooked egg. I could pretend the butter cooks the egg, but that would be wrong. Forget I said anything, though, because your life will be ruined if you don't try this sauce.

1½	**cups heavy cream**
1	**large egg**
1	**"shake" of salt**
1	**cup superfine sugar**
¼	**cup (½ stick) unsalted butter**
2	**tablespoons good rum**
1	**teaspoon vanilla extract**
	Few gratings nutmeg

Whip the cream until it holds soft peaks.

In another bowl, beat the egg with the salt until thick and light in color. Gradually add the sugar, beating until the mixture is thick, light and grit-free.

Melt the butter over very low heat. Cool it slightly while you beat the egg mixture some more.

With a rubber spatula, thoroughly fold the melted butter, rum and vanilla into the beaten egg. Then fold in the whipped cream. Pour the sauce into a serving bowl, decorate it with a few gratings of nutmeg and chill it for at least 1 hour.

Makes 1 scant quart. The traditional way to serve this is to heap a plate with a big scoop of sauce, then drop a few tiny, tiny crumbles of plum pudding on top. For second helpings, it is traditional just to have the sauce.

Powerfully Better Than Any Other Pot Roast

A WELL-MADE POT ROAST is one of those noble, time-honored dishes that—oh, sorry, I forgot I wasn't writing the lyrical kind of cookbook. Still, pot roast is, if not noble, at least something you like to smell when you come into the house on a cold afternoon.

You should use a brisket instead of one of those anonymous "pot roast" cuts at the supermarket. The last time I tried one of those—I think it was called Yankee pot roast—it was like chewing slabs of pencil eraser.

This recipe must be made a day ahead. You'll see why later on.

1	first-cut beef brisket, about 5 pounds, trimmed of all visible fat
	Fresh-ground black pepper
¼	cup corn oil
8	onions, thickly sliced and separated into rings
6	carrots, peeled and cut into chunks
3	cloves garlic, minced
2	bay leaves
4	tablespoons tomato paste
	Salt to taste
1	16-ounce can tomatoes, with juice
1	cup dry red wine

Preheat the oven to 375 degrees F.

Cover both sides of the brisket with lots and lots of pepper. Over a medium flame, heat the oil in a heavy casserole or roasting dish and brown the brisket on all sides. Take the brisket out of the pan and set aside.

Now put the onions in the casserole and cook them over medium-high heat. As you stir them, scrape up the nice brown bits from the bottom of the casserole. Cook the onions for about 15 minutes, or until they are thoroughly brown. Add the carrots, garlic and bay leaves; stir for another minute or so.

Take the casserole off the burner and carefully put the brisket back into its nest of vegetables. Coat the brisket on both sides with tomato paste. Then sprinkle more pepper—and a little salt—over the tomato paste. Pour the tomatoes and the red wine into the bottom of the casserole.

Cover the casserole tightly, first with a layer of foil and then with the lid. Let the pot roast cook on the middle rack of the oven for 3 ½ hours. Check the liquid level in the casserole frequently; if it gets too low, add a little water or beef broth.

When the meat is so tender you can pull off a shred of it without any trouble, take it out of the oven. Keep the meat covered while you cool it to room temperature. Then put it in the refrigerator overnight. This will let you skim the fat out of the sauce.

The next day, spoon off all the solidified fat you can find. Discard the bay leaves. Bring the meat back to room temperature and reheat it—along with its juices and the vegetables—either on top of the stove or in the oven. When it's hot, slice it on the diagonal and serve with the pan juices and vegetables spooned over. You'll probably need to add salt at the table.

Serves 8. This reheats easily, as I guess is already clear.

Modern Potato Salad

PERHAPS "modern" isn't quite the word I want. What I mean here is "Potato Salad in Opposition to Mom-Style." Once again, roasting is the way to go. When you think of all that valuable potato ore leaking out into a pot of boiling water . . . well, just *think* about it!

3	pounds small, unpeeled new potatoes
2	shallots, chopped
1	cup sour cream
⅔	cup mayonnaise
12	slices thick-cut bacon, cooked crisp and crumbled
3	scallions, minced
	Fresh-ground black pepper

Preheat the oven to 350 degrees F.

Spread the potatoes out on a baking pan and scatter the shallots on top. Bake for 20 minutes, or until the potatoes are soft.

Slice the hot potatoes into ½-inch rounds without worrying if some of the skins slip off. Leave the shallots on them, or with them or around them. Put the potatoes and shallots into a mixing bowl.

In a small bowl, combine the sour cream, mayonnaise, bacon and scallions. Pour the dressing over the hot potatoes and stir gently to combine. Add pepper to taste.

Cool the potato salad to room temperature, then chill it overnight.

Serves 8.

Mom-Style Potato Salad

I GOT MY FIRST CATERING JOB when I was in eleventh grade. My assignment: to make a mountain of potato salad and three Jell-O molds. I had never made either before. As a result, I still think of both foods as being scary, hard to make and really impressive.

I hate celery, but I do think it belongs in this salad. I'd miss it if it weren't there. So I've added some to this recipe, which is based on the potato salad in **The Essential Root Vegetable Cookbook** by Martin and Sally Stone.

This must be made 1 day ahead.

2	**pounds Yukon Gold potatoes**
2	**tablespoons corn oil**
1	**tablespoon cider vinegar**
1	**medium Bermuda onion, minced**
1	**stalk celery, minced**
¼	**cup minced fresh parsley**
1	**teaspoon salt**
1	**teaspoon fresh-ground black pepper**
½	**cup cold water**
2	**tablespoons Dijon mustard**
¼	**teaspoon Maggi (a Dutch soup and salad seasoning found next to the Kitchen Bouquet in the supermarket)**
1 ¼	**cups mayonnaise**

Scrub the potatoes and put them into a large pot with enough water to cover. Over high heat, bring the water to a boil. Then turn the heat down, cover the pot and simmer the potatoes for ½ hour. They should be cooked through but still firm. (This may require a few more minutes of cooking. Or a few fewer, if you bought very small potatoes.)

When they're cooked, drain the potatoes, cut them into chunks and put them in a large bowl. While they're still hot, whisk together the oil and the vinegar. Sprinkle this mixture over the warm potatoes, stir them gently and let them cool completely. When they've cooled, combine them with the Bermuda onion, celery, parsley, salt and pepper.

In a small bowl, whisk together the water, mustard and Maggi seasoning. (Don't worry about the water. It's what you need to make the salad creamy.) Whisk in the mayonnaise until the mixture is smooth.

Pour the dressing over the potatoes and their friends, stirring gently until everything is combined. Chill the salad for 24 hours before serving.

Serves 6.

Mashed Potatoes

IN ADDITION to tasting better, mashed baked potatoes are way easier to make than mashed boiled ones because you don't have to peel the potatoes first. The only thing worse than peeling potatoes is peeling shrimp. You don't have to fling big pots of hot water around, either. Just slice open the potatoes, scoop them out into a bowl, and that's it. It's rare that so much less work means so much more flavor.

4	**large baking potatoes**
4	**large cloves garlic, unpeeled**
¼	**cup (½ stick) unsalted butter**
½	**cup heavy cream**
¼	**cup milk**
	Salt to taste

Preheat the oven to 375 degrees F.

Scrub the potatoes well and stab them with one of those potato-baking nails or jam them onto one of those potato-baking torture racks. Or else just pierce them with a fork. (But a potato really does bake better with a nice spike of hot metal inside it.) Place in the oven along with the garlic cloves, which you have previously placed on a little piece of aluminum foil.

After ½ hour of baking, check the garlic cloves. If they're thoroughly softened, take them out of the oven. If not, leave them in for another 15 minutes or so. Once they are out of the oven, squeeze the baked pulp into a bowl and add the butter.

Check the potatoes after 1 ¼ hours. Palpate them a little or stab them with a fork. It's important that they be completely soft in the middle, so keep baking them another 15 minutes or so if you have to.

As soon as the potatoes are done, heat the cream and milk together over medium-low heat. Slice the potatoes open and scrape the contents into the bowl with the garlic and butter. Mash with a potato masher or a big spoon to get the "preliminary lumps" out. Then pour in the hot milk/cream mixture and whip the potatoes with an electric mixer until fluffy. Add the salt and serve immediately.

Serves 4.

Killer Mashed Potatoes

IN **The Essential Root Vegetable Cookbook**, a great book by Martin and Sally Stone, the following recipe appears buried at the bottom of another recipe:

> Unless you were brought up in an Eastern European or Jewish household, you probably have never tasted the most delicious of all mashed potatoes—the ones our mothers used to make mixed with the darkly browned onions and cracklings left from chicken fat. If you don't have an addictive personality and are willing to risk your health to taste one of the most sublime dishes of all time, render about ¼ pound chicken fat with a couple of medium onions, sliced, a small chopped carrot, and a little water, all set over moderately low heat. When the fat has melted completely and the onions are a very dark brown, mix it all, along with a lot of salt and pepper, into hot mashed potatoes. This is living—or its converse if one overindulges.

Reading this recipe may seem almost as delicious as eating the potatoes, but I do urge you to try the real thing just once. Even if you keel over on the spot, you'll die happy.

"I do urge you to try the real thing just once. Even if you keel over on the spot, you'll die happy."

Anita Bryant's Pound Cake

N O ONE CARES about the best pound cake, Mom," my daughter told me when she saw me working on this recipe. Well, I do. My recipe file is stuffed with literally five or six pound cake recipes. "Excellent, better than **Fannie**," I've jotted on the top of one. Another was headed, "Possibly an even better pound cake." But when I got to Anita Bryant's pound cake, I stopped looking.

Her recipe is my favorite so far. The cream isn't quite authentic—real pound cakes are supposed to contain only butter, sugar, eggs and flour—but it does make the cake's texture meltier. When I make one of these pound cakes, I eat it at every meal until it's gone.

The recipe is from **The Anita Bryant Cookbook**, which I discovered 15 years ago in a branch of the New York Public Library. Far more than a cookbook, this is actually the great American novel. It was written back in Anita's Florida Orange Juice days, before all the Dade County stuff, but even so, you can tell how miserable she was with her yucky husband and how hard she was trying to be cheerful. Very plucky stuff.

I *kick* myself for not having stolen this book from the library while I had the chance. I could have just pretended I'd lost it—and reimbursed the library for it—and I would have taken better care of it than anyone else in New York— and the library discarded it long ago, so that proves they didn't even want it—and now it's out of print! I've been looking for a secondhand copy ever since.

I've made a couple of changes in the recipe. One is the addition of a little mace. After all, mace *is* known as "the pound cake spice." I also bake the cake in two buttered-and-floured 9-x-5-inch loaf pans. I just never need one massive pound cake; I'd rather have a second smaller one to stick in the freezer. Also, the cake seems to bake more evenly in two pans than in one.

2 ⅔   cups sugar
8   *medium* eggs, separated, at room temperature, or 7 large eggs
1   pound (4 sticks) unsalted butter, at room temperature
¼   teaspoon salt
3 ½   cups all-purpose flour
⅔   cup light cream or half-and-half
½   teaspoon mace
1   teaspoon vanilla extract

Preheat the oven to 300 degrees F. Butter and flour two 9-x-5-inch loaf pans.

Measure out 6 level tablespoons sugar into a cup or bowl. Beat the egg whites until they begin to form peaks; then gradually beat in the 6 tablespoons sugar. Place this sort-of meringue in the refrigerator until you need it.

In a large bowl, cream the butter well. Gradually beat in the rest of the sugar and the salt; then beat in the egg yolks, two at a time.

Add the flour and the cream alternately to the butter mixture, beginning and ending with the dry ingredients. Add the mace. Whip until the batter is as light as possible, about 10 minutes at medium speed. Then fold in the egg-white mixture and the vanilla. You'll feel as if you're trying to fold egg whites into cement, but persevere.

Pour the batter into the prepared loaf pans. Bake for 50 to 60 minutes, or just until a cake tester stuck in the middle of the cake comes out clean. Cool on a rack for 15 minutes; then invert onto the rack and re-invert onto another rack so the cake will cool right-side-up.

"It should fall 1 inch after taken from oven," says Anita in the book. "This gives desired waxy texture."

Makes two 9-x-5-inch pound cakes.

"I kick myself for not having stolen The Anita Bryant Cookbook from the library."

Puff Pastry

THIS RECIPE can't easily be doubled, but it's easy to make two batches at a time. Everything about this recipe is easy, in fact, and it's fully as good as the classic version.

½   cup (1 stick) unsalted butter
¾   cup sifted all-purpose or bread flour
¼   teaspoon salt
¼   cup ice water

Cut the butter lengthwise into 3 slices and place on a piece of foil and chill. Place the flour and the salt in a bowl and sprinkle the water over, blending with a fork, adding an extra tablespoon of water if necessary so that you can pat the dough into a ball. Put onto a lightly floured board, cover with the bowl and let rest 5 minutes.

Knead until smooth and elastic (about 5 minutes). Roll out to make a neat rectangle about 11 x 6 inches. Position it vertically on the counter so the short end is closest to the counter edge, facing you. Place the slices of butter at even intervals across the top (short end) of the pastry. Fold the bottom half of the pastry up over the butter. Press the edges together firmly. Wrap in foil and chill in the refrigerator for ½ hour or longer.

Unwrap the dough and put onto the pastry board with the fold to your left. Tap with the rolling pin to flatten the dough and roll it into a rectangle 18 x 6 inches, keeping it of even thickness and rolling with long, light strokes. Lift the dough occasionally and dust the board lightly with flour. Fold the left third of the pastry over the center and the right third over the center. Turn the pastry clockwise so that the fold is at the top, and roll out as before. This completes 2 "turns." Repeat until you have made 6 turns, wrapping the dough in floured foil and chilling it for ½ hour after each 2 turns.

Shape, chill and bake according to the recipe.

Makes about ½ pound, enough for about 2 dozen hors d'oeuvres or cookies.

Rice Pudding

. . . is supposed to be a comforting dessert, not a challenging one. Nursery food. That doesn't mean it has to bore you to death, though—which, in turn, doesn't mean you're supposed to gussy it up with a lot of candied fruit and meringue and dabs of jam, as in some recipes I've seen. Whipped cream is the only glamorizer in this recipe.

Make sure you cook the rice enough in the first step. Rice pudding al dente is not a good thing.

2	cups half-and-half
2	cups milk
1 ⅓	cups rice
½	cup plus 2 tablespoons sugar
¼	tcaspoon cinnamon
⅛	teaspoon salt
4	large eggs, well beaten
1	cup raisins, simmered in water for 5 minutes and dried in a paper towel
1	teaspoon vanilla extract
	Several generous gratings fresh nutmeg
1	cup heavy cream

In a double boiler or over very low heat, simmer the half-and-half, milk, rice, sugar, cinnamon and salt until the rice is completely cooked. Stir the mixture frequently—more frequently if you use direct heat, of course. The rice may take ½ hour or longer, making this a good project if you have something else to do in the kitchen.

When the rice is tender, turn the heat way down and stir in the beaten eggs. Stir constantly until the mixture has thickened and resembles a custard rather than a soup, about 2 to 3 minutes. Be sure it never boils.

Let the mixture cool completely. A fast way to do this, if you're impatient, is to put the saucepan in a larger pan of ice water and stir till it's cooled off. When it's cool, stir in the raisins, vanilla and nutmeg.

Now whip the cream until stiff and fold it into the rice mixture. Pour the pudding into a serving dish and chill it for several hours before you serve it.

Serves 6 to 8.

Salad

THIS INFORMATION will change your life. You can order salad over the phone or by mail. It's shipped by two-day UPS and arrives in impeccable shape—fresh, clean and ready to go.

The mixed greens include orach, mizuna and amaranth, none of which I recognized. (Actually, I didn't recognize practically any of the greens.) They come in a dampened brown-paper bag wrapped in plastic. You open the bag, shake them into a bowl and put on some dressing. That's it. Everyone drops dead with amazement.

As of this writing, a pound of greens, containing 20 to 30 different varieties, costs $28, plus $7 for shipping. But it's still less than you'd pay if you tracked down all those different greens. And that's not even factoring in what your time is worth. When you're frantically preparing all the other food for a party, and you know that the salad is not only taken care of but breathtakingly unusual, you'll realize you would cheerfully have paid twice as much.

Northwest Select, 14724 184th Street NE, Arlington, WA 98223. Their phone number is (800) 622-2693.

They take Visa, MasterCard or checks. They also sell edible flowers, garlic wreaths and many other organic wonders.

I love them. I want you to call them up right now.

David's Salad Dressing

THIS IS MY HUSBAND'S SPECIALTY, and our version of house dressing. We do not call it David's Salad Dressing, however; we call it *Manly* Salad Dressing.

All those teaspoons of things may seem pointless when you're reading the recipe, but they work perfectly together. This is a fine-tuned salad dressing.

1	teaspoon egg yolk (Beat the yolk, then measure out a teaspoon.)
1	tablespoon Dijon mustard
1	tablespoon vinegar (David uses manly balsamic.)
1	"shake" Tabasco
1	clove garlic, finely minced
½	cup corn oil
2	teaspoons fresh lemon juice
1	teaspoon heavy cream
	Salt and fresh-ground black pepper

Put that little tiny bit of egg yolk in a small bowl and add the mustard, vinegar, Tabasco and garlic.

Using a wire whisk, beat the ingredients vigorously. Add the oil gradually, still beating. Keep on beating vigorously until the dressing has emulsified.

Add the lemon juice. Beat in the heavy cream. Add salt and pepper to taste. Then retaste to see if you need more mustard or lemon juice.

Makes about ⅔ cup.

Salsa

A S EVERYONE KNOWS, salsa—most improbably—is now outselling ketchup in the United States. I'm not sure why. Maybe it's because people eat more salsa at a time than they do ketchup; maybe it's because McDonald's has started selling Mexican food.

In any case, *this* particular salsa is certainly not the reason. It's too hot for most people. But they are not the people I want to know.

Incidentally, a pepper's seeds are not its main source of heat. Most of the heat comes from the pepper's placenta, the fleshy white thing to which the seeds are attached. (Doesn't a pepper *seem* like the kind of vegetable that would have a placenta?) But the seeds don't add anything in particular to a dish, so you might as well discard them. Along with the placenta, of course.

4	large tomatoes, peeled and chopped coarsely
1	medium onion, minced
2	jalapeño peppers, sliced
1	large clove garlic, minced
5	tablespoons fresh cilantro leaves
2	tablespoons fresh lime juice, or to taste
¼	teaspoon salt

Place all the ingredients in the bowl of a food processor. Using on/off pulses, chop them until they're well blended but not pureed. Taste to see if you need more lime juice or salt. Pour the salsa into a bowl, cover it and chill for at least 2 hours before using.

Makes 2 cups.

Shrimp Salad

FOR LADIES, PREFERABLY. This is an intensely ladylike dish. I mean, *curry powder*, for God's sake! Dried apricots! Still, it always gets eaten and accoladed. And I—well—I—I *like* it.

- 2 pounds medium uncooked shrimp, shelled and deveined
- 1 cup mayonnaise
- 1 cup sour cream
- 3 scallions, finely chopped
- 2 tablespoons fresh lemon juice, or to taste
- 1 tablespoon orange juice
- 2 teaspoons curry powder, or to taste
- ½ teaspoon ground cumin
- ⅔ cup dried apricots, cooked until tender in water to cover, then drained and cut into very small pieces
- 2 bunches of watercress, completely stemmed (All you want is the leaves.) Salt and fresh-ground black pepper

Bring a large pot of salted water to a rolling boil and drop in the shrimp. Cook them for 90 seconds (or just until they are pink, curled and opaque), and then pour them into a colander in the sink. Cool them thoroughly. Dry them with paper towels if necessary.

In a large bowl, whisk together the mayonnaise, sour cream, scallions, citrus juices, curry powder and cumin. Stir in the chopped apricots. Next, gently stir in the shrimp, and last of all the watercress. Correct the seasonings.

Chill the salad for at least 2 hours before serving.

Serves 6 ladies.

Basic Spaghetti Sauce

I DUTIFULLY PLOWED THROUGH batch after batch of homemade tomato sauce, only to realize in the end that I don't *care* about homemade tomato sauce. I don't care about making it myself, I mean. There are some great ones you can buy now. Why bother with all that simmering and all those orange spatters on your stove if you're just going to end up with something that tastes as though it came out of a jar?

Why not highlight the tomato-y-ness of tomatoes instead, rather than their ability to make sauce red? Roasting the tomatoes, onions and garlic does just that, even though roasted vegetables will probably soon be completely unfashionable. (What's next? Maybe deep-fried-tomato sauce.)

I told my friend Jim Paisley that I had a roasted-tomato sauce recipe, and he protested (inaccurately), "You got that from me! That's how I make *my* sauce! Well, that's how I used to make it." Hence the real name of this sauce:

Jim Paisley's Former Tomato Sauce

Bear in mind that the baking part of this recipe takes 3 hours. You may want to make the tomatoes in the morning of the day you plan to serve them.

30	**ripe plum tomatoes, cut in half lengthwise (doing it lengthwise allows for better evaporation of the insides)**
2	**large onions, coarsely chopped**
2	**tablespoons vegetable oil**
4	**large cloves garlic, finely chopped**
2	**pinches sugar**
¼	**teaspoon red-pepper flakes**
1	**pound spaghetti**
8	**slices thick-cut bacon, cooked crisp and crumbled**
½	**cup grated fresh Parmesan**
5	**tablespoons chopped fresh basil**

Preheat the oven to 275 degrees F. Line two large cookie sheets with parchment paper and distribute the tomatoes, gloppy side up, on each cookie sheet.

In a large sauté pan, over low heat, sauté the onions in the oil until softened. Do not let them brown. Sprinkle in the garlic, stir for a minute or so and remove the pan from the heat.

Spoon the onions and garlic over the tomatoes on each cookie sheet. Sprinkle a pinch of sugar over each sheet as well; then sprinkle on the red-pepper flakes.

Bake the vegetables for 3 hours, switching the cookie sheets halfway through the baking so that they'll cook evenly. After baking, cool the tomatoes thoroughly; then peel them. (This is easy to do once they're cool.) Throw away the skins but leave everything else on the trays while you cook the pound of spaghetti that this sauce will cover.

Toss together the hot spaghetti, the vegetables, the bacon, the Parmesan cheese and the basil until everything is well combined. Check the seasoning; then serve immediately.

Serves 4.

Spinach Casserole

CREAM CHEESE is truly a miracle fabric. It lends body and creaminess to countless foods; it can be frozen and thawed and refrozen and rethawed without losing character; and it can be heated without breaking down. In fact, it's really too easy and too convenient to use without being embarrassed. Whenever I cook with it, I'm afraid I seem like a Bake-a-thon contestant.

Still, it's the cream cheese that makes this spinach casserole so good. This is one recipe that tastes much better than it reads, so please try it.

Whenever you use frozen spinach (and as long as I'm feeling embarrassed already, I'll confess that I often do), use frozen *whole* spinach. Frozen chopped spinach gives you much less spinach for the money, and when you try to drain it, tiny, maddening flecks of green get all over everything. Thaw whole spinach instead; squeeze it dry in a dishtowel; and then chop it. It will protect you from that murderous rage that so gets in the way of appreciating a meal.

1½	cups chopped onions
½	cup (1 stick) unsalted butter
1	cup sliced mushrooms
2	cloves garlic, minced
3	10-ounce boxes frozen whole spinach, thawed, drained and squeezed dry in a dishtowel
1	teaspoon Worcestershire sauce
1	8-ounce package Philadelphia Cream Cheese Salt, fresh-ground black pepper, grated nutmeg and cayenne to taste

Preheat the oven to 375 degrees F.

Over medium heat, sauté the onions in the butter until they're translucent. Add the sliced mushrooms and the garlic; continue to cook until the mushrooms—as the somewhat off-putting expression has it—give up their liquid. Add the spinach and Worcestershire sauce and cook for a minute or two. Stir in the cream cheese and seasonings and cook until the cream cheese has melted. Bake in a greased 6-cup casserole for 15 to 20 minutes.

If it's been prepared ahead of time and refrigerated, the casserole should be baked for at least ½ hour. (The mixture can also be frozen unbaked, then brought to room temperature before baking.)

It hardly counts as a vegetable, but this recipe nonetheless makes a nice green statement at a holiday meal.

Serves 6.

Strawberry Pie

I**T VIOLATES** the whole *thing* of a strawberry to cook it. Baked strawberry pie is so flabby! I don't know why anyone bothers with it when they could be eating this instead.

In my house we always have strawberry pie on the first day we go strawberry-picking at the Bronsons' farm. (Actually, we always have two pies—one for dessert, one the next morning for breakfast. We only do it once a year, though.) While we're waiting for the pie to chill, we eat about 10 quarts of other strawberries. Strawberries and raspberries are the only fruits you can't overpick.

You'll need to make this several hours in advance of eating it, but wouldn't you do that anyway?

Pastry
1 cup all-purpose flour
2 tablespoons confectioners' sugar
½ cup (1 stick) unsalted butter, cut in pieces
Pinch salt

Filling
3 ounces Philadelphia cream cheese, softened
½ cup superfine sugar
1 cup heavy cream, whipped until it holds soft peaks
1 tablespoon fresh lemon juice

Topping
1 quart fresh strawberries, hulled
½ cup currant jelly

Pastry: Preheat the oven to 350 degrees F.

Mix all the ingredients together with a pastry blender. Pat them into a buttered 9-inch pie pan. Prick the crust in several places. Bake for 15 to 20 minutes, or until golden brown. Cool thoroughly.

Filling: Whip the filling ingredients together until thoroughly combined. Pour them into the cooled crust, smooth the top and chill for 1 hour.

Topping: Arrange the berries, points up, on the filling. Over low heat, melt the currant jelly. With a pastry brush, carefully paint the berries with the melted jelly.

Sometimes it's hard to fit all the berries onto the filling in one layer. If that's the case, "glue" a second layer on by dipping each berry's stem end in the melted jelly and carefully placing it on the first layer.

Chill the pie for 3 hours before serving.

Makes one 9-inch pie. A more waggish writer would add, "Serves 1 to 2 people."

Strawberry Shortcake
(With a little help from some raspberries)

MAI TAI MOLD. Broken Window Glass Cake. Sierra Snow Cap. Hot Curried Fruit. We have entered the world of desserts as interpreted by one of my favorite cookbooks: **Best Recipes From the Backs of Boxes, Bottles, Cans and Jars**. I don't know that I've ever cooked anything from this book, but I read it compulsively. There's always some new gem waiting to pop out at me.

Shortcake Supreme, for instance. "I've always said that no one could improve an old-fashioned shortcake," claims the author. (*No, you haven't.*) "Well, now I take it all back. This super shortcake is just fabulous. Kraft featured it on their television series and it has gotten rave reviews ever since."

The secret, it turns out, is adding Kraft Marshmallow Creme to the whipped cream you put on top.

This super shortcake really *is* just fabulous. Make sure the berries are cold and the biscuits are hot.

Berries
1	10-ounce bag sweetened frozen raspberries, defrosted
1	quart ripe strawberries, hulled and sliced in half (save 8 good-looking berries to use whole as garnish)

Shortcake Biscuits
2	cups cake flour
¼	cup sugar
4	teaspoons baking powder
½	teaspoon salt
½	teaspoon cream of tartar
½	cup (1 stick) unsalted butter, chilled and cut into 8 slices
½	cup milk plus ½ cup heavy cream, combined in the same measuring cup
½	teaspoon vanilla extract

Topping
1 ½ cups heavy cream
¼ cup sugar
1 teaspoon vanilla extract

2 tablespoons unsalted butter

Berries: Force the raspberries through a fine sieve into a bowl to remove their seeds. Whisk the puree and juice to blend them, and then pour them over the strawberries. Chill the berries for 2 hours, stirring once or twice.

Biscuits: Preheat the oven to 400 degrees F. Lightly butter a 9-x-13-inch baking pan.

In a food processor, blend the cake flour, sugar, baking powder, salt and cream of tartar. (Put your hand over the pouring tube to keep flour from floating into the air.) Add the butter and pulse the mixture on and off until the mixture resembles fine bread crumbs.

Transfer the flour mixture into a bowl and stir in enough of the milk-cream mixture and the vanilla to produce a soft dough. (You'll need at least ⅔ to ¾ cup of liquid.) Turn the dough out onto a floured surface and knead it gently for a few seconds.

Roll the dough out ¾ inch thick. Cut out 8 shortcake-sized rounds. You should use all the dough. Place the shortcakes on the prepared baking pan with their sides slightly touching. They don't fill the whole pan, so I always make a fake pan side of aluminum foil to put against the "open edge" of the biscuits. Bake the shortcakes for 20 minutes, or until lightly browned.

Topping: While they're baking, whip the heavy cream until it begins to hold its shape; add the sugar and vanilla, and continue to beat until the cream forms soft peaks. Cover the bowl and stick it in the fridge.

Assembling the shortcakes: When the shortcakes are done, let them cool for a couple of minutes before removing them from the baking pan. While they stand, melt the 2 tablespoons of butter. Slice the shortcakes in half and lightly brush their interiors with melted butter. Place the bottom of each shortcake on a dessert plate. Divide half the berries among the plates; top with the top half of each shortcake; top that with more berries; and finally pile on the whipped cream. Set a whole berry on top of each whipped cream mountain.

Serve immediately to 8 people who are *so* happy not to be eating marshmallow creme.

"Serve immediately to 8 people who are *so* happy not to be eating marshmallow creme."

Corn Bread-Pecan Stuffing

To START WITH, you will need to make some corn bread. May I suggest the recipe on page 93? To make corn bread for stuffing, though, you should use only half the sugar in the recipe.

1	pound best-quality bulk breakfast sausage
1	cup finely chopped onions
½	pound mushrooms, very finely chopped (a food processor works well for this)
2	large cloves garlic, minced
1	teaspoon dried thyme
¼	teaspoon dried sage
¼	pound chicken livers, cut into very small pieces (Don't worry. They won't wreck the whole thing. They'll just add an indefinably perfect quality.)
½	cup chopped fresh parsley
2	large eggs, well beaten
3	cups crumbled corn bread
1	cup pecans, toasted at 350 degrees until crisp, then chopped coarsely Salt and fresh-ground black pepper

In a large, heavy skillet, over medium heat, cook the sausage until it is well browned. Keep breaking it up with your spoon as you stir. With a slotted spoon, put the sausage into a bowl and drain all but 2 tablespoons fat from the skillet.

Add the onions to the skillet, and cook until they begin to wilt. Add the mushrooms, garlic, thyme and sage. Cook until the mushrooms give up their liquid; then continue cooking until the liquid evaporates. Add the chicken livers and parsley, and cook until the livers turn pink. Add the sausage to the skillet again, mixing well. Take the skillet off the heat and add, in order, the eggs, corn bread crumbs and pecans. Season to taste. Store the stuffing in the refrigerator until you're ready to cook the turkey.

Makes enough to stuff a small turkey—say, under 12 pounds—or a capon or a large roasting chicken (with some left over).

Wild Rice Stuffing

FOR WHEN you suddenly go a little mad and jettison all your old ways.

- **1 large onion, chopped**
- **2 shallots, chopped**
- **6 tablespoons unsalted butter, melted and cooled**
- **4 cups cooked wild rice, preferably cooked in chicken stock (1 cup raw rice)**
- **1½ cups fresh cranberries, picked over, coarsely chopped**
- **⅓ cup Lyle's Golden Syrup (available at specialty stores and some supermarkets in the honey-and-molasses section, or substitute 3 tablespoons dark corn syrup plus 3 tablespoons light corn syrup)**
- **1 tablespoon fresh rosemary leaves, chopped**
- **½ teaspoon salt, or to taste**
- **½ teaspoon fresh-ground black pepper**
- **8 slices thick-cut bacon, cooked crisp and crumbled**

In a large saucepan, over medium heat, sauté the onion and shallots in the butter until softened and lightly browned, about 10 minutes. Add the cooked rice, cranberries, Golden Syrup, rosemary, salt and pepper, and cook, stirring, for 10 minutes. Remove the pan from the heat, stir in the bacon and adjust the seasonings. Store the stuffing in the refrigerator until you're ready to cook the turkey.

Makes about 5 cups, enough for a 10-pound turkey.

Another Really Great Stuffing With Sausage In It

I HOPE THAT IN MY LIFETIME it will become acceptable to admit that Pepperidge Farm can make better stuffing than regular people can. Better than I can, anyway. For many years I followed my mother's example and made two stuffings at Thanksgiving: one grown-up stuffing with, say, homemade rye bread cubes and, oh, *let's try raw almonds and uncured olives this year!*; and one kid stuffing with Pepperidge Farm mix and apples and browned onions. Even when there *were* no children at the table (and believe me, I didn't mess around making two stuffings once there were children at the table), the Pepperidge Farm-based stuffing usually disappeared first.

I guess the sage-scented breath of truth must have been abroad in the land. At about the same time I had the Pepperidge Farm Revelation, so did many other food writers—including Sarah Leah Chase, author of the wonderful **Nantucket Open House Cookbook** and creator of my favorite stuffing recipe. I've tinkered with Chase's recipe a bit, but not because it really *needed* tinkering with.

I try not to feel too embarrassed about relying on a convenience food during a major national holiday. After all, there are many other Pepperidge Farm recipes with which no mortal would presume to toy. When's the last time you whipped up your own batch of Milanos?

3	cups diced dried apricots
¼	cup amaretto liqueur
¾	cup Poire William liqueur
1½	cups (3 sticks) unsalted butter
1	very large yellow onion, chopped
1	bunch scallions, sliced (both white and green parts)
1½	pounds Pepperidge Farm herb stuffing crumbs
1	pound sweet Italian sausage, casings removed
12	ounces bulk pork sausage

2   **ripe pears, cored and diced**
3   **tablespoons chopped fresh rosemary leaves**
3   **cups water**
      Salt and fresh-ground black pepper

Soak the apricots in the amaretto and ½ cup of the Poire William for 2 hours.

In a large skillet, over medium-high heat, melt 1 ½ sticks of the butter. Add the onion and scallions and cook, stirring occasionally, for 10 minutes. Transfer the veggies to a very big bowl and introduce them to the stuffing crumbs.

Add the two kinds of sausage to the same skillet and cook, crumbling the meat with your spoon, over medium-high heat, until the mixture is no longer pink. Add the meat to the bowl and stir everything. Add the pears and the rosemary, and restir. Add the apricots and their liquid, and stir.

In a small saucepan, heat the remaining 1 ½ sticks of butter with the water until the butter is melted. Pour the butter-water and the remaining ¼ cup of Poire William over the stuffing mixture. Mix well. Check the seasoning and add salt and pepper to taste.

Store the stuffing in the refrigerator until you're ready to cook the turkey. (You do know that you should never prestuff a turkey, right?) Any stuffing that doesn't fit inside the turkey can be baked, covered, at 350 degrees F for 40 minutes.

This makes enough to stuff a 22- to 24-pound turkey. Also, Sarah Leah and I like to eat it straight.

"I try not to feel too embarrassed about relying on a convenience food during a major national holiday."

185

Sugar Cookies

NOT TO SOUND LIKE you-know-who, but I've been collecting cookie cutters since I was a child. In my family's opinion, a house without millions of kinds of cookie cutters is like a house without toilet paper. Cactuses, shamrocks, witches' brooms, Santa's heads that look more like a bag of potatoes—we have them all. Most often we use them for these rolled sugar cookies.

The secret to these cookies is rolling them out so thinly that transporting them anywhere will make you faint with nervousness. These were always the cookies my mother would make for school parties when I was little. I don't know how she ever *got* them to the parties; *I* certainly never let them out of the house.

Dusting the work surface and the rolling pin with confectioners' sugar instead of flour helps keep the cookies even more delicate, another trick my mother discovered. Thanks, Moomskidii.

1	cup (2 sticks) unsalted butter, at room temperature
2	cups sugar
2	large eggs
1	teaspoon vanilla extract
2	tablespoons milk
3½	cups all-purpose flour
2	teaspoons baking powder
½	teaspoon salt
	Confectioners' sugar

Cream the butter and the sugar together until light. Add the eggs and the vanilla. Beat until fluffy, and add the milk. In a separate bowl, sift together the flour, baking powder and salt two times. Beat the flour mixture into the butter mixture until well mixed. Then wrap the dough in wax paper or plastic wrap and chill it for at least 1 hour.

Preheat the oven to 375 degrees F and butter some cookie sheets. (If you want to be even more like my mother, you can butter every cookie sheet in your house and use them one after another. This saves preparation time, if not washing time.)

Break off a hunk of dough from the refrigerator, dispensing pinches of it liberally to anyone in the kitchen. Dust your rolling surface, your rolling pin and the hunk of dough with confectioners' sugar. Roll the dough out to ⅛-inch thinness—or even thinner, if you can bear to—cut out with cookie cutters, place on greased sheets and bake for about 8 minutes, or until faintly browned around the edges.

Cool on racks.

Makes about 200 cookies.

Real Cream of Tomato Soup

THIS IS THE REAL ITEM. Unfortunately, for it to be at its best requires your making it in summer, when tomatoes are at *their* best. (Although the tomato base cooks for a reasonable length of time, no amount of reduction can mask wan, flavorless tomatoes.)

½	cup (1 stick) unsalted butter
1	pound onions, thinly sliced (about 2 cups)
4	pounds ripe tomatoes (about 20 medium), cored
1	teaspoon dried basil leaves
	Large pinch cayenne
2	cups heavy cream
⅓	cup brandy
	Salt and fresh-ground black pepper
	Fresh basil for garnish

Melt the butter in a large, heavy pot. Add the onions and cook them over medium-high heat until they're limp and beginning to turn golden. Coarsely chop the tomatoes and add them, together with any juice, to the onions. Stir in the dried basil and cayenne. Cook, uncovered, over medium-high heat for 30 minutes.

Force the mixture through a sieve or pass it through a food mill that is fitted with a medium blade. Turn it into a clean, nonaluminum pot or large saucepan. Warm gently.

Scald the cream and stir it thoroughly into the tomato mixture. Heat through (do not boil) and stir in the brandy. Add salt and pepper to taste. To serve, garnish with large, perfect leaves of basil.

Serves 8.

Roast Turkey

SOMETIMES in New Orleans they serve deep-fried whole turkey. How festive! Luckily you can make a roast turkey look just as cracklingly brown as a deep-fried one without having to buy a 50-gallon fry kettle. Brush this basting sauce on your turkey and you'll automatically recreate that Norman Rockwell painting called "Free From Want."

Of course, for a really gorgeous appearance you should leave the turkey raw and paint it with a mixture of corn syrup and Angostura bitters. That's what food stylists do to keep turkeys in photographs from looking shriveled.

Back to our own turkey, though. It may seem like a lot of trouble to turn over a whole turkey partway through the baking. And really, it *is* a lot of trouble. But it means that the whole bottom half of the turkey becomes usable meat instead of pallid-skinned sludge. It also means that the breast meat stays moister. And it means that your Thanksgiving guests get to hear lots of swears fly out of the kitchen as you try to wrestle a burning-hot turkey to the ground.

1	fresh or defrosted turkey
	Corn oil
½	cup (1 stick) unsalted butter
½	cup turkey or chicken stock
	Juice from 1 large lemon
2	tablespoons Worcestershire sauce

Preheat the oven to 325 degrees F. Take that little bag of giblets out of the turkey's body cavity. Either cook them up for the dog or make them into (yuck) giblet gravy. Rinse the turkey in cold water and pat it completely dry with paper towels.

Place a pie pan filled with hot water on the bottom oven rack. Refill it as needed while the turkey cooks.

Stuff the turkey's cavity and neck. Flip the wings backwards to pin down the neck skin. Sew up the cavity opening; the best way to do this is with a large-eyed needle threaded with dental floss. Use more floss to truss the legs together.

Take a huge sheet of parchment paper and fold it several times so that it will fit in your roasting rack with 6 to 8 inches of overhang on each side.

Brush the turkey breast with corn oil. Upend the turkey and place it breast-side down in the roasting rack. With a mighty burst of energy, heave the roasting pan into the oven.

Now, make the basting sauce: In a small saucepan, over low heat, combine the butter, turkey or chicken stock, lemon juice and Worcestershire sauce. After the first hour of roasting, you're going to be basting the turkey top and bottom with this mixture every 15 minutes or so. About halfway through the baking, you'll be able to start swiping up some pan juices with the basting brush and using them to baste with as well.

Bake the turkey for 15 minutes a pound if it weighs less than 16 pounds. If it weighs more than that, bake it for 12 minutes a pound. Similarly, turn it breast-side up after 1 hour if it weighs less than 12 pounds, and after 1 ½ hours if it weighs more. You'll almost certainly need another person to help you do this. Sometimes my husband and I sort of flip the turkey with pancake turners. Sometimes he puts on a pair of rubber gloves and just lifts it up with his hands. So far he's never dropped it.

When the turkey is done, a meat thermometer inserted in the breast will read 170 degrees F; inserted in the thickest part of the thigh, it will read 180 to 185 degrees. Leave the turkey covered on the top of the stove for 15 minutes before you carve it.

Vanilla Ice Cream

THIS RECIPE makes store-bought superpremium vanilla ice cream taste like water. But you do have to make it two days before you plan to use it. If you serve it before it's hardened, it will seem much too rich. Of course it will be just as rich when it's thoroughly chilled, but since you don't notice, you won't care as much.

        2   vanilla beans
        4   cups heavy cream
        8   large egg yolks
       ⅔   cup sugar, preferably superfine
             Pinch salt

On Day One, cut vanilla beans in half lengthwise. Place the heavy cream in a heavy nonaluminum saucepan and scrape the seeds into the cream. Drop the pods into the cream as well and chill the mixture overnight.

On Day Two, in a medium bowl, whisk the egg yolks, sugar and salt together until light. Meanwhile, scald the cream; then fish out the vanilla pods and discard them. (Leave the seeds in the cream, of course.) Very gradually whisk the cream into the egg-yolk mixture. You want to combine the mixtures thoroughly, but not make them foamy. When combined, transfer the mixture—now a custard—to the saucepan.

Over very low heat, and stirring constantly, cook the custard for 6 to 8 minutes. (If you have a candy thermometer, the custard should reach 170 to 180 degrees F.) As soon as it begins to thicken, remove it from the heat. Cool the custard, then chill it thoroughly. I do this by carefully placing the saucepan into a larger pan of ice water and stirring until the mixture is cold, about 20 minutes. If you use the refrigerator, it will take several hours to chill the mixture thoroughly.

Transfer the custard to an ice-cream maker and freeze it according to the manufacturer's directions. Then transfer the custard—now ice cream, of course—to a sealed container. Leave it in your (regular) freezer overnight to mellow the flavor and firm the texture.

This recipe makes 1 quart. Serve tiny portions until you're used to it. About the size of butter pats would be good.

A couple of excellent variants:

Cinnamon Ice Cream: On Day One, use just 1 vanilla bean. Along with the scraped-out vanilla bean, add 3 whole cinnamon sticks to the cream. On Day Two, remove the vanilla pod and the cinnamon sticks and stir 1 teaspoon of cinnamon into the cream. Proceed as for Vanilla Ice Cream.

Nutmeg Ice Cream: Once again, use only 1 vanilla bean. Along with it, add 3 whole nutmegs to the cream. The next day, after fishing out the nutmegs and the vanilla pod, stir 1 freshly grated nutmeg into the cream. (The ones you've been soaking will be too soft and wet to grate.) Proceed as for Vanilla Ice Cream.

Both Cinnamon and Nutmeg Ice Creams are great on apple pie (pages 15 and 18).

My Only Vinaigrette

I KNOW, I KNOW: there's too much vinegar. It's too strong. It will over-power the subtle flavor of more delicate greens. The thing is, though, that I almost always serve more *assertive* greens that stand up to this vinaigrette very well. And I've certainly never had any complaints when I've used it on plain old lettuce.

It's a very simple recipe except, perhaps, for the Maggi seasoning. One always used to see Maggi next to the Kitchen Bouquet; it's not there as often now. But it's worth seeking out when you find yourself in a really big super-market or a specialty store. A jot of it makes vinaigrettes seem mysteriously un-copy-able—and that, of course, is always pleasant for a cook.

6	tablespoons corn oil
3	tablespoons balsamic vinegar
1 ½	tablespoons Dijon mustard
½	teaspoon Maggi seasoning

Whisk everything forcefully together until it emulsifies.

Makes a little over ½ cup—enough to coat greens for 4 to 6 people.

Watermelon Sorbet

THIS IS UNQUESTIONABLY the best way to serve watermelon. You'll need an ice-cream maker.

1	cup sugar
¾	cup water
3 ½	cups chopped, seeded watermelon pulp
⅓	cup fresh lemon juice
2	tablespoons cassis liqueur
	A few watermelon seeds for decoration

Over high heat, combine the sugar and water in a small saucepan. Stir constantly until the syrup boils; then lower the heat, cover the pan and boil the syrup gently for 4 minutes. Cool, then chill. You'll use all the syrup in this recipe.

Puree the watermelon in batches in a food processor or blender. You need 2 ½ cups; if you don't have enough, chop up a little more watermelon.

Combine the pureed watermelon with the thoroughly chilled sugar syrup, the lemon juice and the cassis. Pour it into your ice-cream maker and freeze it according to the manufacturer's directions.

When you serve this sorbet (and it's best served immediately), sprinkle each serving with a few watermelon seeds for cuteness.

Makes 1 quart.

Country Braid (White Bread)

ANOTHER RECIPE given to me by Rebecca Atwater, who is a veritable *font* of good recipes. If you prefer, instead of making braided loaves, you can make two conventional loaves and bake them in two greased bread pans for about 40 minutes.

2	packages active dry yeast
½	cup lukewarm water
1	teaspoon plus ½ cup sugar
¼	teaspoon ginger
5	cups bread flour
½	cup dried skim milk (must be skim)
1	cup warm water
¼	cup (½ stick) unsalted butter, melted
2	large eggs, well beaten
1	teaspoon salt
1	large egg yolk, beaten with 1 teaspoon water

Combine the yeast, ½ cup lukewarm water, 1 teaspoon sugar and ginger in a small bowl and let sit in a warm place until the yeast is bubbling. In a large bowl, mix 2 cups of the bread flour, the dried skim milk, the 1 cup warm water and the remaining ½ cup sugar. Add the yeast mixture and beat well until combined.

Stir in the butter, the eggs, salt and remaining 3 cups of bread flour. Knead the dough for 10 minutes, or until smooth and elastic. Return it to the bowl, which you have washed and buttered. Cover the bowl with a damp dishtowel and let the dough stand in a warm place until double in bulk, about 45 minutes to 1 ½ hours.

Turn the dough out of the bowl. With floured kitchen scissors, cut it into 3 equal pieces. Cut each of them into 3 equal pieces. With your hands, roll each piece out into an 18-inch-long rope. Braid 3 ropes into a loaf and pinch the ends together, tucking them under the loaf. Repeat, making 3 braided loaves in all. Place 2 of the loaves on a buttered cookie sheet and the third on another. Cover them with the damp cloth (or cloths) again, and again let them rise until double. When you can see that they're almost there, preheat the oven to 375 degrees F.

Paint the loaves with the egg-yolk wash and bake them for 20 minutes. Cool on racks. Unless you plan to eat the bread within a day, it should be frozen.

Makes 3 braided loaves.

White Chocolate-Raspberry Pie: The Best (Nay, Only) Use for White Chocolate

THIS MAY BE the best dessert in the world. It's certainly my daughter Laura's favorite. When she was six, she wrote her own version of the recipe, which read as follows:

4 squares of bitter chocolate
some buttercream
one bag of raspberries
plan crust

Melt the bitter chocolate. Smush the raspberries. Make the crust. First put the raspberries in the crust. Then buttercream. Then freeze it. Then it is done.

Laura was wrong about one thing. This recipe doesn't freeze well at all; the raspberry filling goes all kerflooey. (Generally, sauces and fillings containing cornstarch can't be frozen.) But you can make parts of it ahead of time if you want to. I'd recommend it, because the pie is rather labor-intensive to do all at once. The crust (which *can* be frozen) can be made a few days in advance, as can the raspberry filling (which should be refrigerated).

Note that there are uncooked eggs in this pie. For a while I worried about what to do with uncooked eggs in this book. Finally I decided it would be enough to warn people about them. I've fed this pie to lots and lots of people, and they're all still with us.

Tart Shell
1½ cups all-purpose flour
1 tablespoon sugar
¼ teaspoon salt
¾ cup (1½ sticks) unsalted butter, chilled and cut into 10-12 slices
¼ cup ice water
½ teaspoon vanilla extract

Raspberry Filling
- 1   12-ounce bag *unsweetened* frozen raspberries, thawed
- 1   tablespoon fresh lemon juice
- 3   tablespoons sugar
- 2   tablespoons cornstarch

White Chocolate Buttercream *(reserve ½ cup for optional garnish)*
- 4   ounces white chocolate, coarsely chopped
- ½   cup (1 stick) unsalted butter, *at room temperature*
- ¼   cup superfine sugar
-     Pinch salt
- 2   large eggs, *at room temperature*
- ½   teaspoon vanilla extract

Note: If the eggs or butter are too cold, you will end up with a gloppy mess.

Chocolate Glaze
- 2   ounces bittersweet chocolate, coarsely chopped
- 2   ounces unsweetened chocolate, coarsely chopped
- ¼   cup (½ stick) unsalted butter

Garnish (optional)
- 10   fresh raspberries
-     Reserved ½ cup white chocolate buttercream

Tart shell: Butter the sides and bottom of an 11-inch round fluted tart pan with a removable bottom.

In the bowl of a food processor fitted with a steel blade, place the flour, the sugar and the salt. Pulse the processor on and off a few times to blend the dry ingredients. Drop the sliced butter on top of the dry ingredients and pulse about 20 times, or until the mixture resembles cornmeal. Combine the water and vanilla extract in a small bowl. With the processor motor running, pour the water mixture through the feed tube. Process just until the dough forms a ball.

Divide the ball of dough into 4 roughly equal portions and place them in the buttered tart pan, spacing them evenly. Using your fingertips, press the dough evenly into the tart pan. The dough should be slightly thicker around the sides and should extend about ¼ inch above the top of the pan.

Chill the dough for 1 hour. Then preheat the oven to 375 degrees F. Lightly butter one side of a 14-inch square of aluminum foil and place it, buttered-side down, on the unbaked tart shell. With a fork, prick through the foil (and the tart shell, of course) in 12 places on the bottom and 8 places on the sides. Then fill the foil with 2 cups of aluminum pie weights, raw rice or dried beans, spreading them evenly.

Bake the tart shell for 20 to 25 minutes, or until the edges are slightly browned. Carefully lift out the foil and whatever you've weighted it with, and bake the shell for about 10 minutes more, or until it is entirely golden brown.

Cool the shell on a rack, leaving it in the pan.

Raspberry filling: Strain the thawed raspberries through a fine sieve a little at a time, pausing frequently to dump out the seeds. Stir the lemon juice into the pureed raspberries.

In a small nonaluminum saucepan, stir together the sugar and the cornstarch. Then thoroughly whisk in the raspberry puree. Cook the mixture over medium heat, stirring constantly, until it reaches a full rolling boil. Continue to boil the mixture, stirring, for 5 seconds, then remove it from the heat. Don't taste too much of it—you really need it all.

If you're making the raspberry filling the day before you make the tart, cool it to room temperature; then cover it with plastic wrap and chill overnight. If you're making it on the day you plan to use it, stir over iced water until chilled. *Then* cover it with plastic wrap and chill it.

White chocolate buttercream: In the top of a double boiler over hot water—neither boiling nor simmering—stir the white chocolate until it is two-thirds melted. Then remove from over the hot water and stir until thoroughly melted. White chocolate gets very nasty when it's overheated, and this will help keep it from seizing. If the chocolate isn't already tepid, cool it until it is.

In the small bowl of a standing mixer, or in a medium bowl with a hand-held mixer, cream the butter and sugar together for 5 minutes. Gradually beat in the tepid white chocolate and the salt. Add the eggs, one at a time, beating the mixture until fluffy after each egg. Beat in the vanilla extract. Set aside ½ cup of the mixture to garnish the tart, if you plan to do so.

It will all go easier if you leave the tart in the tart pan for now.

Spread the chilled raspberry filling evenly across the bottom of the baked tart shell. (One of those half-width rubber scrapers works well for this.) Spread the white chocolate buttercream across the raspberry layer. Be sure you extend the buttercream all the way to the edges; don't leave any raspberry filling showing.

Chill the tart for 30 minutes to firm the buttercream layer.

> "I've fed this pie to lots and lots of people, and they're all still with us."

Chocolate glaze: In the top of a double boiler, over barely simmering water, stir together the chocolates and the butter until they're mostly melted. Then remove from the heat and stir until fully melted. Cool for 5 minutes. Take the tart out of the fridge.

Pour the chocolate glaze over the buttercream, tilting the tart pan back and forth until it's thoroughly coated. (It doesn't matter if some glaze drips over the sides.) If that makes you too nervous, you can spread the glaze with a spatula.

Chill the tart yet again. If you plan to garnish it, place the reserved ½ cup buttercream in a pastry bag or a pastry tube fitted with a star tip. Pipe 10 evenly spaced rosettes around the edge of the tart, and top each rosette with a (perfectly dry, so it won't smear) fresh raspberry.

Or you can just do the rosettes. Or you can just eat the buttercream with a spoon. When I'm pressed for time, I melt about 3 ounces of white chocolate, dip my finger in and repeatedly shake my finger over the tart. This makes a sort of scribbly pattern that I like to think looks high-tech.

Return the tart to the refrigerator until serving time.

About ½ hour before serving, remove the tart from the refrigerator and take it out of its tin. Then set it on a serving plate and leave at room temperature until the rest of the ½ hour is over.

Serves 6 to 8, depending on seconds requested.

Whole-Wheat Bread

THE BASIS FOR THIS excellent recipe comes from Jane Brody's **Good Food Book**. When I was pregnant with my first child, I ate this bread every day, often washing it down with some dreadful mixed-vegetable juice I bought at a health-food store near my office. The beets made the juice a yucky purplish brown. (I don't remember what I ate when I was pregnant with my second child.) I've made a few changes in the recipe, but the main credit goes to Jane Brody as well as to her husband, who invented the recipe.

½   cup dry wheat berries
2   cups water
2   cups milk
6   tablespoons butter plus 1 tablespoon melted butter for brushing loaves
⅓   cup light brown sugar, packed, or honey
2   teaspoons salt
½   cup lukewarm water
2   packages active dry yeast
½   teaspoon sugar
2   large eggs, well beaten
1   cup old-fashioned rolled oats
½   cup bran flakes (unprocessed bran)
3   cups whole-wheat flour
3   cups bread flour
½   cup wheat germ, toasted with honey

Put the wheat berries and the water into a medium saucepan. Simmer them for 2 ½ to 3 hours, adding more water if necessary. (You can work on the bread at the same time, of course. You don't have to sit there looking at the stove.)

Scald the milk. Pour it into a large mixing bowl and add the butter, brown sugar or honey and salt. Let the mixture cool to lukewarm.

Pour the lukewarm water into a small bowl. Stir in the yeast and the sugar, and let the mixture proof for 10 minutes.

When the yeast is bubbly and the milk mixture has cooled to lukewarm, combine the two. Stir in the beaten eggs. Then stir in the rolled oats and the bran flakes.

If you're a wuss, like me, transfer the mixture to the large bowl of your electric mixer and attach the dough hook at this point. Or transfer it to your food processor (you may have to do it in batches, depending on the processor's size). Or roll up your sleeves and start kneading. Whichever method you choose, add all the whole-wheat flour and as much of the bread flour as you need to make the dough easy to handle. It should be slightly moist but not sticky.

Beat, knead or process the dough until it is smooth and elastic, adding more bread flour if necessary. (In an electric mixer with the dough hook, this will take 6 to 8 minutes; by hand, about 10 minutes, and in a food processor, 2 to 3 minutes.)

Put the dough into a buttered bowl. Turn it a few times to coat it with the butter. Cover it with a damp dishtowel or with plastic wrap, and let it rise in a warm place until it has doubled in bulk (about 1 ½ to 2 hours).

Punch down the dough. Either return it to the mixer or roll up your sleeves again. (The food processor won't work for this step.) Check the wheat berries to see if they're easy to chew; drain them well and pat them dry with a paper towel; then work them thoroughly into the dough.

Form the dough into 3 equal parts. Shape them into loaves and put the loaves into buttered 9-x-5-inch bread pans. Cover the pans and put them in a warm place until the dough has once again doubled in bulk.

Preheat the oven to 350 degrees F.

Brush the tops of the loaves with the remaining 1 tablespoon melted butter and sprinkle them with the wheat germ. Put them in the oven and immediately turn the heat down to 325 degrees.

Bake the loaves for 35 to 40 minutes, or until they sound hollow when you thump the bottom of the loaves.

Makes 3 largish loaves.

Zucchini-Parmesan Bread

To ME, sweet zucchini breads are nothing more than a way to use up excess zucchini. And if, like me, you don't have a vegetable garden—I hate digging, and I hate the way those big, floppy leaves look, and besides the deer would eat everything—you don't have a problem with 900 boat-sized zucchini anyway.

Then along came this recipe in Jane Brody's **Good Food Book**. Of course I had to doctor it a little to bring up the fat content suitably. Jane Brody has such a way of cheating us of our fat!

1½	cups whole-wheat flour
1½	cups all-purpose flour
1	cup grated Parmesan
⅓	cup sugar
5	teaspoons baking powder
½	teaspoon baking soda
¼	teaspoon salt
¼	teaspoon fresh-ground black pepper
1	cup shredded, unpeeled zucchini, squeezed dry in a towel
1	cup buttermilk
½	cup (1 stick) unsalted butter, melted and cooled
2	large eggs, lightly beaten
2	tablespoons grated onion

Preheat the oven to 350 degrees F. Butter and flour a 9-x-5-inch loaf pan.

In a large bowl, mix together the flours, Parmesan, sugar, baking powder, baking soda, salt and pepper. Mix in the zucchini.

In a small bowl, combine the buttermilk, butter, eggs and onion. Add this liquid mixture to the flour mixture and stir well. Pour the batter into the prepared loaf pan.

Bake the bread for 55 to 60 minutes, or until a tester inserted in the middle of the loaf comes out clean.

Cool the bread for 20 minutes before turning it out onto a rack to finish cooling.

Makes one 9-x-5-inch loaf.

Leftovers

Apples, what kind to use. It's maddening the way recipes call for apples you can't possibly find unless you're on the way to an old-variety orchard in October. "A firm-fleshed, tart apple will work best in this recipe," they inform you solemnly, "such as a Northern Spy, Gravenstein, Ashmead's Kernel, King of Tompkins County or Belle de Boskoop." Sure, it's fun listing old apple names (hey, here are some more! Maiden's Blush! Mammoth Black Twig! Sops of Wine! Monstreuse D'Amerique! Blue Permain!), but it doesn't do the average cook much good. When I can get Chenango Strawberry or Winter Banana or Black Gilliflower or Vittles and Drink apples, I use them; failing that, I go for Granny Smiths without feeling guilty. Grannies are very juicy, so if I'm using them in a pie I add more cornstarch than I would with, say, a McIntosh or an Esopus Spitzberg. (Okay, I'll stop.)

Bacon, why this book contains so much. I wish bacon were treated with the reverence it deserves: as a more-valuable-than-gold flavoring agent rather than the greasy killer most educated people believe it to be. My feeling is that *every* main dish is better if you add some bacon. Maybe someday I'll even start leaving the main dish part out and just serving the bacon. To soften the blow, I might call it "salad." After all, Jell-O is sometimes called salad in the Midwest.

Baking powder, baking soda and other little bits of dry ingredients, how to keep track of them as you add them. Like the mental patient I once read about who compulsively asked himself, "Have I pushed anyone into the elevator well?" I'm always wondering, "Have I put in the baking soda and baking powder and spices, and if I haven't, which ones have I left out?" It's no use putting each mystery ingredient away as I use it, because I never remember to do that. So what I do now is drop each teaspoon and quarter-teaspoon and eighth-teaspoon in a different place on top of the batter. Then I can count and see what's missing before I start beating again.

Butter, to soften quickly. You've heard all the other ways: shredding it into a warmed bowl, cutting it very thin, sticking it in the microwave so that the inside remains rock-hard and the outside is all melty. What the hint books don't tell you is that putting a (wrapped) stick of butter into your pants pocket softens it quickly, too. You might not want to do this when company is around, but your family won't care.

Buttering pans. Actually, Crisco works better for greasing pans than butter. It gives more coverage. But I can't stand it. I don't want my lovely fragile doughs and batters coming into contact with Crisco. So I butter my pans rather lavishly. (I save butter wrappers in the freezer for just this purpose.) When there's the slightest doubt that something will come out of the pan, I butter it, line the bottom with parchment, butter the parchment, and then flour the parchment and sides of the pan as well. Haste can make lots and lots of waste if you let it.

Cake layers, keeping them level. You *have* to use Magi-Cake Strips, which are metallic fabric strips you moisten and wrap around your cake pans before baking. They keep the sides of the pan cooler, thus maintaining a uniform rate of baking and preventing overbrowning. I had read about them, but never believed they worked until my friend Bill Fairbairn showed me a maple cake as miraculously even as a Styrofoam mold. Magi-Cake Strips can be ordered from Maid of Scandinavia (see page 208).

Cardboard, Christmas uses. It may sound heretical, but you can make a much better gingerbread house if you don't use any gingerbread. Just make your house out of corrugated cardboard and tape it together. Then frost it completely—it won't look very festive if people can *see* that you've used cardboard—and decorate it as usual. Since most families don't eat the bread part of the house anyway, nothing is lost except about 500 opportunities to swear you'll never bake a stupid gingerbread house again.

As long as we're on the topic of gingerbread houses, two other hints. If you have very young children, assemble the house (cardboard or gingerbread) the night before you give it to them to decorate. Few kids can happily sit through the baking-and-assembly stages of a gingerbread house, especially because you, as chief architect, are likely to be tense at this time. Your children will be much more interested in the part of the process that involves globbing on frosting and sticking on five pounds of gumdrops.

The other hint: If making a gingerbread house is a big Christmas deal at your house, try saving the project until a few days *after* Christmas Day. It's nice for kids to have something to look forward to once post-Christmas gloom sets in.

Oh, and Andes Mints make nice roof shingles
We have wandered away from C, I see.

Cheese, temperature of. It bears repeating that cheese tastes a lot better at room temperature. It bears remembering that it takes several hours to *get* cheese to room temperature. If you're serving it before dinner, take it out of the fridge at lunch. Keep it wrapped, of course.

Chocolate, my abridged history of. Careful readers will have noticed that I use a lot of chocolate. It's easier for me than for some people because I buy chocolate in 50-pound boxes. I switched to this method once I read Jennifer Lang's **Tastings**. In this great book, which I'm very jealous I didn't write, Lang and a test panel blind-tested various foods—canned tomatoes, vanilla, sardines, tea—and then rated them. They tested a whole range of chocolates. Some didn't do too well. ("Cheesy, sharp, strong aftertaste," was one grade. "Sweet, tastes like suntan lotion," was another.) But Merckens chocolate rated best in both the Semisweet and Milk categories, beating out Tobler, Lindt and Droste varieties.

So I called Merckens and found out the name of the distributor closest to my house. Then I called him—his name was Armand DeNoyer—and placed what must be one of his smallest orders. Ever since then he's been very kind about delivering my hundred pounds of semisweet Yucatan Vanilla Buttons each fall. "Buttons" are oversized chocolate chips. Not only do they turn regular chocolate-chip cookies into glorious gloriousities, but they're also easier to use than the big five-kilo blocks I used to buy and chop up with an ice pick. The only drawback to Yucatan Buttons is that they're too easy to eat handfuls of.

Merckens' 800 number is (800) 637-2536.

Chocolate, unsweetened. The **Tastings** testers also rated unsweetened chocolate. (They didn't eat it straight; they made it into mousses.) Anyone who buys chocolate in grocery stores will be dismayed to hear that the testers rated both of the standard grocery-store unsweetened chocolates unacceptable. And it's true that both these chocolates seem awfully dusty and dry and sour-smelling when you break them apart.

All is not lost, however. Malleable soul that I am, I immediately stopped using regular unsweetened chocolates once I'd read **Tastings**. But I didn't have much trouble finding replacements. The little grocery store in my town sells Ghirardelli unsweetened chocolate that's very good, and I sometimes order a five-kilo block of Callebaut unsweetened chocolate from Maid of Scandinavia. (See page 208.) If you're luckier than I, you might be able to figure out how to find Nestlé's "Peter No. 23" variety, which was the **Tastings** testers' favorite. I've never been able to persuade anyone at Nestlé's to sell me some.

Cream Cheese, why I only use Philadelphia. Because it's the best brand, and it never varies. Some of the more upscale cream cheeses are too soft and squishy to work with, though you might prefer them over Philadelphia if you're making your own herbed cheese or something.

Crisco, how to measure. Once in a while you do have to use Crisco. It is the best vegetable shortening for pie crusts. You can keep reminding yourself what a good skin cream it is, but that doesn't make it any easier to touch the stuff. The best way to measure Crisco without smearing it all over the kitchen is to pack it into a tablespoon and level it off with a knife—a knife you then use to scrape the Crisco into the bowl. No matter how many tablespoons you use, this is still easier than mashing the Crisco into a cup or using the displacement method and squishing Crisco-y water all over the counter.

Luckily, none of the recipes in this book call for more than a few tablespoons anyway.

Dental floss, uses for. It's supposed to be perfect for cutting a cheesecake. You take a long piece of floss, hold it out on either side of the cake, and then pull it down through the cake. But then you reach the crust, which doesn't yield in quite the same soft, squidgy way. What I do is to use the floss to cut the cheesecake part of the slice; then I switch to a spatula to get the crust out. It's not perfect, but it's less messy than using a spatula alone.

Dental floss works very well for trussing a chicken or turkey, though. Thread a big-eyed needle with floss and sew up the bird's cavity like a little pair of pants. Dental floss is also good for tying the chicken's fat little legs together. Just don't use the mint- or cinnamon-flavored kind.

Garlic, potency of. I'm sure you know all the arguments against using a garlic press. One thing you may not have heard, though, is that pressing garlic makes the garlic ten times more potent than mincing it. I love garlic, but I don't want it leaping out of bounds unless I've given it permission. I've learned to mince it with a big knife, and you should too.

One way to make the mincing process less tedious is to do lots and lots of garlic in the food processor. (Okay, it's tedious peeling all those cloves, but you have to do *some* work in this life.) Mince 10 heads of garlic at once, roll them up into a log inside plastic wrap and freeze them. Then, whenever you need minced garlic for a dish, you can just chip off the right amount with a spoon. You don't need to thaw it before using, either.

Ginger, speaking of freezing things. When you buy a knob of ginger, chop it into 1-inch chunks and freeze them. If a recipe calls for minced ginger, just pull out a hunk of frozen ginger, chop off the peel with a heavy knife and grate it on a grater. (As opposed to grating it on a bicycle.) Again, you don't need to thaw it. Just grate it and go.

Grapes, how to set up. The instant you get a bunch of grapes into your house, wash it and cut it into little clusters. That way, people can help themselves to a cluster instead of picking single grapes off the stem and leaving horrible, wormish, twisted, naked stems in the bowl. This is helpful advice if the sight of a wrecked-up bunch of grapes gives you as many heart attacks as it does me.

Herbs and spices, which ones to buy. The absolute best come from a mail-order place called Select Origins, 11-10 Old Dock Road, Yaphank, NY

11980. Outside New York, call (800) 822-2092. Inside New York, call (516) 924-5447. Select Origins also sells excellent dried cherries—the yuppie raisin replacement—in bulk, as well as high-quality rices, olive oils, liquid cilantro and many other things. It's worth being on their mailing list.

If you can't bring yourself to buy spices by mail-order, at least make sure that the ones you buy in the supermarket are packaged in glass jars, not plastic. Manufacturers put their highest-grade herbs and spices into glass.

Date your spices when you get them home. (I write the date with a laundry marker on top of the lid.) When an herb or spice turns six months old, force yourself to toss it. This really *is* important, and I really do it; I replace a few jars each week so the cost won't seem so staggering. (If you doubt that it makes much difference, sniff an old jar and a new jar next to each other.)

The only jars I don't throw out are the ones I never use, like chervil. It makes me feel pleasantly housewifeish to see lots of spices all lined up in my spice box. If I happen to come across a good-sounding recipe that calls for chervil or some other arcane herb, *then* I go out and buy a new bottle.

Maid of Scandinavia, the essential catalog. I've been waiting a long time to use the word "compendium." Not only does this company sell practically every baker's and confectioner's supply in the world, but it also sells tiny plastic graduates' heads to stick into cakes; tiny plastic First-Communion boys and girls, for the same purpose; citric acid, for those who make their own hard candy; malic acid, for those who make their own apple-flavored hard candy; black food coloring; and gold dragees the size of thumbs. This is one catalog you can't be without. Write them at 3244 Raleigh Avenue, Minneapolis, MN 55416; call them at (612) 927-7996.

Mayonnaise. I'm just not going to tell you to go out and make your own mayonnaise all the time, no matter how much respect you lose for me. Let's be honest. Homemade is preferable when you're eating it straight or nearly straight—as a topping for shrimp, say—but it's too bland and rich-tasting for everyday fare. (Food writers have to throw in the word "fare" once in a while.)

Bottled mayo is wonderfully easy to dress up. Adding some lemon juice makes it taste much more homemade. (Try adding some tomato paste, grated orange rind and chopped scallions when you're making rice salad.) It lasts a lot longer than the 10 days that is the maximum storage time for homemade. In other words, don't feel bad about using store-bought mayonnaise unless you love making mayonnaise. *Do* feel bad about using "salad dressing," though.

Molasses, pouring. Grease the measuring cup first, and every drop of molasses will slide out. I keep a spray can of Pam for this kind of operation. A friend of mine saw it and said incredulously, "What do you use *Pam* for?" Since then I've kept the can hidden in the liquor cupboard.

Muffin papers, necessity for. You absolutely should use muffin papers every time you make cupcakes or muffins. You'll spare yourself a lot of heartache. And you may think you're wasting paper, but what about all the soap and water you waste washing those muffin tins?

Mushrooms, washing. Just for the record, it's fine to wash mushrooms. It does not make them absorb water. Don't use soap, though.

Olive oil, why there isn't any in this book, except for in the Lentil Soup recipe, where I will grudgingly allow it. Because I hate it. The better quality it is, the more I hate it. I hate celery too.

Peel, candied. This crucial plum-pudding ingredient usually tastes like sugared asphalt shingles. But it's almost Christmas. Do you really have the time to make your own? If not, you can buy Australian Glacé Lemon Peel and Australian Glacé Orange Peel from Williams-Sonoma. I'll let the catalog do the talking for me: "Slightly sweetened with pure cane sugar, these moist peels enliven baking with their fresh citrus tang." They enliven steaming too. Williams-Sonoma's number is (800) 541-2233. Their address is P. O. Box 7456, San Francisco, CA 94120-7456.

Rubber spatulas. Most people don't own enough of these. You should have at least five on hand; it will make life a lot simpler. It's not a bad idea to put a band of masking tape around one rubber spatula and reserve that one for working with beaten egg whites. Rubber spatulas get greasy easily, and grease—as we should all know by now—keeps egg whites from rising.

Salt, adding a pinch of it to everything. Add a pinch of salt to everything. Desserts too.

Saran Wrap, superiority of. As Bounty is the best paper towel, so Saran Wrap is the best plastic wrap. And it's thick enough that you don't waste time clawing it off the roll.

Tomatoes, whole canned. American brands are often better than Italian. Don't be fooled by foreign writing on the label.

You wouldn't want to slice up a canned tomato for a salad, but most of the fresh, ripe tomatoes on the market are so bland and woolly and generally awful that whole canned tomatoes work better in recipes.

Vanilla, why you're making a mistake when you buy supermarket brands. Here, too, Jennifer Lang took me by the hand and gently steered me in the right direction. By far the best vanilla flavoring is La Cuisine's Vanilla Essence. It comes in teeny little bottles, but it's very concentrated. I use it in recipes where a pure vanilla flavor is of paramount importance: vanilla ice cream, for instance, or eggnog or pound cake. In recipes where I don't have to use the absolute all-time best ever, I use an extremely good second best: Nielsen-Massey's Madagascar Vanilla Extract, which you can get from Williams-Sonoma (see "Peel," page 209, for their address). I buy this extract by the quart and stick a couple of slit vanilla beans in the bottle to juice it up even more. I'm sorry to lean so heavily on Jennifer Lang, but she is a goddess to me.

La Cuisine: 323 Cameron Street, Alexandria, VA 22314. Telephone: (703) 836-4435.

Index

C